Water-Based Finishes

Water-Based Finishes

ANDY CHARRON

The Taunton Press

Cover photo: Scott Phillips

Printed in the United States of America
10 9 8 7 6 5 4 3 2 1

The Taunton Press, Inc., 63 South Main Street,
PO Box 5506, Newtown, CT 06470-5506
e-mail: tp@taunton.com

Distributed by Publishers Group West

Library of Congress Cataloging-in-Publication Data

Charron, Andy.
    Water based finishes / Andy Charron.
        p.   cm.
    Includes index.
    ISBN 1-56158-236-0
    1. Wood finishing. 2. Finishes and finishing. I. Title.
TT325.C497   1998
684'.084—dc21   98-6988
                                                      CIP

To my mother, Anne,
and to the memory of my father, Ernest.

Acknowledgments

A great number of people assisted in the creation of this book. In particular, I would like to thank all of the people at The Taunton Press, including Joanne Renna, Rick Peters, Helen Albert, and Diane Sinitsky.

Thanks also to Chris Minick, whose comments and insights proved invaluable, and to Ed Kelly, who took all of the photographs in this book.

In addition, several manufacturers' representatives provided a wealth of valuable information. The following people deserve thanks for graciously giving their time and resources: John McKee and Greg Penn of Sherwin Williams; Joan Goldberg at Hydrocote; Teresa Morgan and Les Spangenberg of Eclectic Products; Tom Monahan of General Finishes; Mary Shomon of the National Paint and Coatings Association; Gary Driscoll of Basic Coatings; and David Fuhr of FSM Corp.

Finally, thanks to Bob Grause of Ivy Woodcraft and Michael Wilson of Wilson Woodworking for their assistance in preparing for the photographs, and to my wife Anne and son Brian for their help and encouragement.

Contents

Introduction

My first experience with water-based finishes came about purely by accident. Several years ago, I was building a small entertainment center for a customer. I used a hand-rubbed oil finish on the visible parts of the cabinet and shellac on the interior sections and drawers. I'd just begun finishing the drawer boxes when I ran out of shellac. As I was heading out to buy more, a friend of mine, who happened to be a professional painter, pulled up the drive. When I explained where I was going, he pulled a can out of the back of his van. "Try this, you'll like it," he said, handing me a gallon of something I had never seen before. "It dries fast, sands easily, and doesn't smell. Best of all, it cleans up with water!" I'm just finishing drawers, I thought, so what have I got to lose? I thanked him, grabbed the can, and proceeded to brush on two coats of finish in a few hours.

This "new" product turned out to be a water-based urethane that had, unbeknownst to me, been on the market for several years. I was satisfied with the results, but the finish did have a few problems that concerned me. Not only did it raise the grain severely but it also tended to bubble and foam as I brushed it on. Although it sanded fairly easily, I felt that the combination of raised grain and trapped air bubbles made me work harder to get a smooth finish. I kept the can on hand and used it as an occasional substitute for shellac, but I never viewed it as a replacement for my usual finishing methods.

A few years later all that changed. I had just purchased my first spray gun but did not have the space or funds for an explosion-proof booth. By now I was a little more familiar with water-based finishes, and I knew I could spray them in my small shop. This time I tried a new product that was billed as a "water-based lacquer." I was amazed at how easy it was to use. Although it still raised the grain, it was much less of a problem than the water-based product I'd used before. The finish flowed out nicely and dried to the touch in minutes.

Because I couldn't safely use flammable products in my shop, I had no choice but to use water-based finishes. Gradually I figured out ways to overcome each of the problems associated with these products, while developing a simple, consistent finishing schedule. Today I use a variety of products in my shop, including both solvent- and water-based systems, although I would estimate that 90% of the time I use water-based finishes.

As the demand for cleaner, safer, more environmentally friendly products increases, more and more people are turning to water-based finishes. As a result, in just the past few years the number of products available has increased dramatically. In fact, just about every major finish manufacturer now offers a complete line of water-based products, many of which are equal to or even superior to traditional solvent-based finishes. However, after talking with several woodworkers, I realized that when it comes to water-based materials, there is a lot of misinformation floating around. I frequently hear people complain that water-based products are too expensive, are hard to work with, don't withstand abuse, don't dry properly, and require special equipment. Unfortunately, most of the books on wood finishing available today devote only a few pages or a short chapter to water-based products. I have written this book to expand the volume of information available to anyone thinking of using water-based finishes and to answer some of the often erroneous charges leveled against them.

In this book, I examine all aspects of water-based finishes, including an overview of how these products were developed. Other chapters explain how the different types of water-based finishes work, while helping unravel some of the mysteries surrounding the various names and types of materials. I discuss the advantages of water-based products along with some of their disadvantages. I realize that not all finishes are right for every situation, so it is my hope that by understanding the pros and cons of water-based finishes you'll be better able to determine when and what to use.

The heart of the book examines the types of water-based products available and how to apply them. Beginning with fillers and putties and moving through sealers, stains, dyes, clear topcoats, and opaque finishes, each material is discussed in detail. Topics include appropriate surface preparation, proper equipment and shop conditions, application techniques, and finish maintenance. Then I show just how easy it is to clean up after using water-based products. Finally, because things don't always go as planned, a detailed troubleshooting chart is included to help you avoid and overcome potential finishing problems.

Most of what I have learned about water-based finishes comes from talking to manufacturers, finishing specialists, and other woodworkers, along with a lot of trial and error. Throughout the book, I draw on my real-life experiences to answer frequently asked questions while offering helpful hints and tricks that make using these finishes easier. I hope that the knowledge, information, and experiences presented in this book will help you achieve satisfactory results quickly and consistently with little effort and frustration.

1

Why Use Water-Based Finishes?

One day I was talking with the owner of a local cabinet shop and he mentioned the problems he was having with his finishing operation. His building is on the edge of a residential area, and the neighbors were complaining to the local authorities about the smells coming from his shop. "Whenever I spray lacquer," he lamented, "the health inspector shows up and makes me stop."

"Why not switch to water-based products?" I asked. "They are nonflammable, nontoxic, and odorless. In fact, I've been using them almost exclusively for more than six years and haven't had even one encounter with the local officials."

"I tried a water-based lacquer once," he groaned, "but it didn't work."

He was never really able to explain why the water-based finish didn't work, but I suspect the main reason was because he didn't give it a *chance* to

work. Rather than spend the time learning the right way to apply these finishes, he simply tried it once, didn't like the results, and gave up. The last I heard he had grown tired of fighting with his neighbors and is now sending all of his pieces to be finished elsewhere.

Stories like this are not uncommon among professional woodworkers. Many people who have been using the same materials and methods for years are reluctant to switch to a new technology, especially if they feel it is inferior to what they are comfortable with. Fortunately, I began using water-based products early enough in my career that I hadn't yet become dependent on one type of finish. I quickly realized that water-based materials are not difficult to apply or "worse" than traditional finishes; they are just "different." In fact, I feel that for the average woodworker, water-based products are equal to or even superior to many solvent-based materials. I will not go so far as to say they are the perfect finish, for I don't think that exists. However, I do feel that the benefits offered by water-based products are strong enough to warrant their use under most conditions.

Advantages of water-based finishes

Chances are if you are reading this book, you are considering using a water-based finish on a project. In case you need more convincing, I have listed here, in no particular order, the main reasons to use these finishes.

FAST BUILDING

The key ingredient in any finish is the resin, or solid, that dries to form the final film. The more solids a finish contains, the thicker the dry film will be. A typical water-based finish derives about 35% (and some as much as 50%) of its weight from solids, whereas most traditional lacquers have a solid content of 20% to 25% or even lower. The higher solids content of water-based products helps the finish build faster, thus requiring fewer coats. For example, most spray finishes are designed to be applied in a wet coating of 4 mils thick. If the coating contains 20% solids, the dry film that remains after the solvents evaporate will be 0.8 mils thick. When a finish containing 35% solids is applied 4 mils thick, the resulting dried finish will be 1.4 mils thick. It follows that three coats of a water-based finish would build to 4.2 mils, while it would take at least five coats of a traditional lacquer to build the same film.

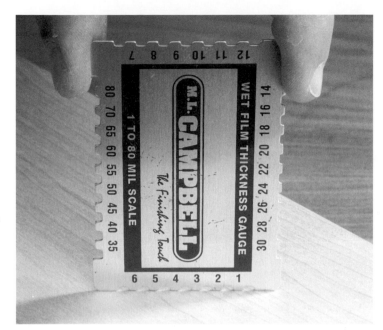

A film thickness gauge is a quick way to measure the thickness of a wet coating. Counting the marks made by the gauge will tell you how many mils thick the wet finish is.

This high solids content gives water-based finishes a real advantage over traditional lacquers. Since you can apply fewer coats, you don't have to work as hard to finish a project. You spend less time applying the finish, sanding between coats, and cleaning up. Best of all, fewer coats means you use less material. Although a gallon of water-based finish may cost more than a gallon of varnish or lacquer, you use less to cover the same area, so you actually save money.

NONFLAMMABLE

To see if water-based products really are nonflammable, I once lit a small fire in a metal pail and poured a can of water-based lacquer on it. The liquid put out the flame just as if I had doused it with plain water. If you do not have a spray booth with an explosion-proof fan and

When using water-based finishes, you do not need an expensive spray booth. A small fan and an open window or door should provide plenty of air circulation.

vapor-tight lights, you will certainly appreciate the fact that water-based products are nonflammable. All you need to spray or brush them is a clean area with good ventilation. This makes water-based products the ideal choice for someone who is finishing in a garage or basement that may contain a furnace or water heater.

SAFE FOR YOU AND THE ENVIRONMENT

Although water-based finishes do contain small amounts of toxic solvents, the amount is insignificant when compared with traditional finishes. Less solvents in the finish means prolonged exposure is not as hazardous, which is of special consideration for professional cabinetmakers and production shops and is one of the reasons I use these finishes today. When I occasionally have to use nitrocellulose lacquer on a project, I am irritable or have a headache by the end of the day, even though I have a spray booth and wear a respirator. When working with water-based finishes under the same conditions, I can spray all day and feel no different than when I started. Plus, because these finishes use water as the primary cleaning solvent, exposure to toxic materials is even further reduced.

Water-based materials were developed as part of the search to find finishes that would help reduce environmental pollution. The fact that water-based finishes contain less dangerous materials means they are not only better for you but also better for the environment.

One word of caution: Although water-based products are nontoxic, which basically means they won't kill you if you drink them, keep in mind that too much exposure to anything is not good for you. While it is true that water-based finishes don't contain the high amounts of chemicals found in solvent-based products, they still contain some solvents that can be harmful if inhaled in large or repeated doses. If you use a spray gun to apply these finishes, you should always wear a good-quality respirator. If you only work in the finishing room on occasion and brush all your finishes, you don't need to take any special precautions when working with water-based products. Good ventilation is all you need.

NO NEED FOR EXPENSIVE EQUIPMENT

The fact that water-based finishes are nonflammable means you can use them in situations where solvent-based materials would be unsafe. Although you should always have good ventilation when doing any kind of finishing, you don't need explosion-proof fans as you would when working with solvent-based materials. All you need is a regular house fan and an open window or two. Lighting and electrical fixtures in and around your finishing room do not have to be explosion-proof or even vapor-tight. Also, if you keep a lot of cans of finish on hand, as most professional shops do, you don't need an expensive, explosion-proof metal cabinet for storage. Setting up a properly equipped spray booth or finishing room for traditional lacquers can be an expensive proposition, all of which can be avoided simply by using water-based finishes.

FAST DRYING

One of my favorite reasons for using water-based finishes is that they dry fast, especially when compared with brushable varnishes and polyurethanes. Most manufacturers say that when their finishes are applied under ideal conditions (35% humidity, 70°F), they will dry to the touch in 15 to 30 minutes and can be sanded and recoated within 2 hours. I have found that these times are extremely conservative. In most cases, a typical water-based coating will be dry to the touch in 5 to 10 minutes and can be handled, sanded, and recoated within an hour. If you spray finish, you will find that drying times for water-based finishes are comparable to those of traditional lacquers and shellac. However, if you brush on your finishes,

If you use traditional lacquers and varnishes, you may have to invest in a large, expensive fireproof cabinet like the ones pictured here.

The "fast-drying" oil-based polyurethane on the left takes 2 to 4 hours to dry to the touch, compared with 10 to 15 minutes for the water-based product on the right.

the drying times for water-based finishes can't be beat. I have yet to see a solvent-based, brush-on finish that dries as fast as a water-based product. Even so-called "fast-dry" polyurethanes take at least an hour to dry to the touch and many more hours before they can be sanded and recoated.

The fast-drying properties of water-based finishes give them definite advantages over solvent-based products, especially when applying them by brush. First, because they dry so quickly, the chances of dust settling into the wet finish is significantly reduced. This means you can achieve a better finish with less work and the working environment doesn't have to be absolutely spotless to get a good finish. Also, multiple coats of fast-drying finish can be applied quickly. Under the right conditions, it is not unusual to apply three or four coats of finish in one day.

This is especially helpful if you do your finishing in the same room as your sawing and sanding. The amount of "down time" lost while you are finishing a piece is greatly reduced.

CLEAR DRYING AND NONYELLOWING

The exceptional clarity of most water-based products makes them the ideal choice when you want the finish to protect the wood but not change its color. I have used water-based finishes with great success over pickled, painted, and colored furniture. I also like to use water-based topcoats when I am trying to match a difficult shade of stain. Once I have the color of the stain right, I don't want to worry about the topcoat changing its shade by making it darker or more amber in tone. Also, water-based finishes won't yellow with age the way most lacquers and varnishes do, which makes them a good choice for finishing light-colored woods like ash and maple.

DURABLE AND SCRATCH RESISTANT

The resins used in water-based finishes have improved to the point where most products are at least as durable, if not more so, than solvent-based materials. In fact, the water-based lacquers I use in my shop are all approved for use on furniture and cabinets by the Kitchen Cabinet Manufacturers Association (KCMA). These products form a tough, flexible film that is highly scratch resistant and can withstand most forms of abuse, including heat, alcohol, and most common household foods and chemicals.

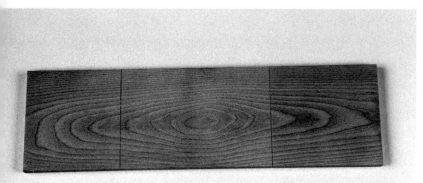

Water-based finishes are ideal for "pickled" or light-colored woods. The solvent-based coating on the right makes the whitewashed finish look dark and yellow, while the water-based finish on the left causes very little change.

EASY TO CLEAN

I have yet to meet anyone who actually enjoys cleaning up after a long day of spraying or painting. Running a spray gun or brush through several washes of smelly, toxic solvents is not a pleasant task. However, the cleaning solvent for water-based finishes is warm, soapy water, which helps make the clean-up process safer and less of a chore. (For more on cleaning up, see Chapter 10.)

Disadvantages of water-based finishes

As far as I know, there is no such thing as the perfect finish. While a topcoat may be ideal in one situation, it may be inappropriate in another. Unfortunately, this is also true of water-based finishes. Although the reasons to use them may make them sound like the best finishes on the market, they do have some drawbacks. Understanding what these potential pitfalls are and how to overcome them will make the choice of whether to use water-based finishes easier.

SENSITIVITY TO WEATHER

Perhaps the biggest cause for concern when using water-based finishes is the one thing we have the least control over: the weather. I mentioned that water-based finishes dry fast under ideal conditions. However, under conditions that are less than ideal, water-based finishes can be difficult to apply. The two worst conditions under which you can use water-based finishes involve high humidity and cold temperatures. In my part of the country, it is not unusual to have summer days with 90°F temperatures and 98% humidity. Under these conditions, finishes that would normally be dry to the touch in 5 to 10 minutes may be wet for 30 minutes or more. And even more frustrating, they may not be ready to sand for 3 to 4 hours. This not only slows down production but also means there is more time for dust or other contaminants to land on the soft, wet finish.

Cold, damp winter days have the same effect on water-based finishes as do heat and humidity. If the finish (or the piece being finished) is cold, the finish will not flow and level properly and will dry with a mottled, textured look. When spraying, the material will come out in thick drops rather than in a fine mist, and orange peel will be a problem. When brushing, the material will be difficult to flow on the surface, and brush and lap marks may not level out and disappear.

If you live in the Southwest, you probably have close to ideal conditions most of the year. However, the rest of us may be lucky to have two or three months a year with days of 35% humidity and 70°F temperatures. That does not mean that we cannot use water-based products. In fact, by taking a few precautions, I regularly apply these finishes on cold winter days and throughout the hot, humid summer months. The trick on a cold day is to be sure the finishing room or area and the piece being finished are as warm as possible. But it is even more important to be sure the *finish* is warm. A warm finish is easier to brush or spray, and it flows, levels, and dries much better and quicker than a cold finish.

Submerging a can of finish in a bucket filled with hot water will warm the finish and help it flow better and dry quicker.

Taking the chill out of a cold finish begins with where the can is stored. Never keep water-based products in an unheated garage during winter months and keep them off cold concrete floors. Water-based finishes will freeze, becoming useless once they do.

Warming a finish is quick and easy to do. By simply placing the can in a container of hot water, it will quickly warm up to a usable temperature. On cold days in my shop, I place a gallon can of finish in an empty 5-gallon container and pour in enough hot water to nearly submerge the can. I use water straight from the tap, but you could heat the water on a stove if you want to warm the finish more or faster. (Never heat the finish itself directly on a stove or over a

flame. Although water-based products are nonflammable, it is a bad idea to begin the practice of placing *any* finishing material where it could create a fire hazard.)

I have found that leaving a can of finish in a bucket of warm water for 10 to 15 minutes is usually enough to bring it to a workable temperature. Ideally you want to bring a finish up to around 70° to 75°F. However, warming a finish does not have to be an exact science. You will know that a finish is still too cold if it handles poorly. If so, simply warm it some more. Getting a finish too warm should not be a problem if you are spraying, but it could make brushing more difficult by speeding up the drying time.

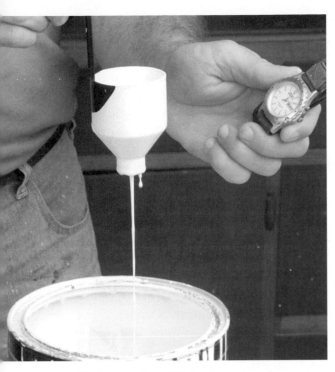

Timing how long it takes for a viscosity cup to empty will give you a good idea as to whether your finish is the right consistency for spraying.

If you prefer to have precise control over the finish-warming process, you could either use a thermometer to check its temperature or use a viscosity cup to measure how well the finish flows. If you know how fast the finish should flow through the cup at the ideal temperature, simply warm it until it flows at the proper rate. (For more on viscosity, see Chapter 8.)

Finally, on cold winter days, it is important to keep warm air moving over the piece after it has been finished. A strategically placed fan is all you need to ensure proper airflow. This will not only help the finish flow and level better but will also speed up the drying time.

Compensating for the elements on a hot, humid summer day is a bit more of a challenge than simply heating the room

or raising the temperature of the finish. The best way to overcome the effects of high humidity is to remove moisture from the air. Sounds simple, right? If you are working in a relatively small, tightly sealed room, this may not be too much of a problem. A good-quality dehumidifier (or two) can be used to reduce the humidity in the room enough to where drying time is not noticeably slowed down. However, if your finishing area is a large basement, open garage, or backyard, removing moisture from the air may be impractical, if not downright impossible.

This does not mean you cannot use water-based finishes on humid days. I have found that by increasing the amount of air flowing through the room, and particularly the air flowing over the piece as it dries, I am able to partially offset the effects of high humidity. I do this by turning on an extra fan or two in my finishing room after the piece has been sprayed. Increasing the amount of air moving over the piece as it dries helps the water in the finish evaporate more quickly than it would if left sitting in a roomful of damp, stagnant air. Although a few extra fans will not completely eliminate the negative effects of high humidity, keeping a large amount of fresh air circulating through the room should help lower drying time to acceptable levels.

GRAIN RAISING

One of the biggest complaints I hear from fellow woodworkers regarding water-based finishes is that they raise the grain so much that you spend more time sanding than you would with a traditional, solvent-based finish. When I first started using water-based finishes, I would have agreed with them. However,

Some water-based products may not adhere to solvent-based finishes. This flooring sample was coated with rubbing oil and then sprayed with a water-based lacquer. The dry finish scraped off the surface without too much effort.

SPECIAL SPRAY EQUIPMENT

Another common argument I hear for why people don't want to use water-based finishes is that they think you need special equipment, especially if you are using a spray gun. It is true that your spray equipment should ideally be made of plastic or stainless steel, otherwise it may begin to rust or corrode. However, lack of the right type of gun doesn't mean you can't spray water-based products—you just have to be more careful. As long as you get your gun completely dry at the end of the day, you should be able to spray water-based products with no problem. (See Chapters 8 and 10 for more on this topic.)

NONCOMPATIBILITY WITH OTHER FINISHES

Another potential problem that must be considered when using water-based products is their compatibility with fillers, stains, dyes, and other topcoats. If you've ever tried to mix oil and water you know what happens: No matter how much you shake or stir, the two just won't mix. The same thing may happen if you try to lay a coat of water-based material over an oil-based product. The water-based topcoat may not adhere to the surface. Sometimes this problem shows up immediately, while other times it may take a day or two for the two materials to separate. Although this is not as much of a problem as it was a few years ago, it is still something that must be taken very seriously when combining water-based finishes with other products.

A coat of dewaxed shellac or an appropriate sealer is usually enough to ensure compatibility between two

as the formulas used in water-based products have improved, the amount of grain being raised has at best been nearly eliminated and at worst been reduced to what I consider acceptable levels. I consider "acceptable levels" of grain raising to be just that: an amount of raised grain that I can eliminate without any undue use of time or energy. Under normal circumstances, any finish you apply will need to be sanded between the first and second coat. Some, like traditional lacquer, may need very little sanding, while others, like shellac, raise the grain and need to be thoroughly smoothed out before applying another coat. I consider this first sanding step necessary regardless of the type of finish, so as long as I'm not working overly hard to prepare the surface for the next coat, raised grain does not bother me. (See Chapter 8 for tips on dealing with raised grain.)

Water-based finishes at a glance

Pros

- Due to high solids content, finishes build fast, requiring fewer coats.

- Nonflammable.

- Safer for you and the environment.

- Don't require spray booths or explosion-proof fixtures.

- Dry fast.

- Film is clear, nonyellowing, durable, and scratch resistant.

- Easy to clean up.

Cons

- Sensitive to weather.

- Raise grain.

- Spray equipment must be kept clean and dry.

- Potential compatibility problems over solvent-based products.

dissimilar materials, but the only way to be sure you won't have a problem is to test the finish on a scrap piece of wood first.

Should you use water-based finishes?

Now that I have outlined the pros and cons of water-based finishes, you are probably wondering if and when you should use them. Although I am obviously a big fan of these products, I will be the first to admit they may not be right for everybody all the time. Recognizing when they are a good choice and when they should be avoided is the first step on the road to successful application of these types of finishes.

WHEN ARE WATER-BASED FINISHES APPROPRIATE?

As far as I'm concerned, water-based finishes are appropriate in just about any situation imaginable. If you need a hard, scratch-resistant finish that is easy to apply and dries fast, they would be a good choice. If you are looking for a clear, nonyellowing finish for light-colored woods or "pickled" furniture, water-based products are for you. If you want to spray your finishes but don't have a proper spray booth or good ventilation, then nontoxic, nonflammable water-based products are the safest choice.

Because water-based finishes are nontoxic, they are not only safer for you and the environment but are also a good choice for finishing children's furniture and toys. Also, the low-odor, high scratch-resistance, fast-drying characteristics of water-based products make them ideal for wood floors.

WHEN ARE WATER-BASED FINISHES INAPPROPRIATE?

Although I like to use water-based products whenever possible, there are three occasions when I would opt for something else. The first involves high-production situations. Occasionally, I am asked to finish large quantities of something for a customer. They usually need the finish to match another part and want it done in a hurry. For example, I was recently asked to refinish 180 pieces of ¼-in.-thick hardboard that measured 32 in. wide by 6 ft. long. The factory in Canada had done a beautiful job of painting the smooth side with a white, solvent-based lacquer. Unfortunately, the panels were supposed to be gray. My customer asked me if I could refinish the panels the proper color and have them back to him in two days.

I tried spraying a coat of water-based pigmented lacquer over the previously finished surface, but the bond between the two products was not very good. If I wanted to use my usual water-based coatings, I would have had to turn the panels over and finish the bare back side. I was looking at several hours of spraying primer, followed by a ton of sanding, and more work applying the topcoat. Instead, I decided to spray on one coat of a production-grade nitrocellulose lacquer over the previously finished surface. The final results were what my customer wanted, used half as much material, and took one day instead of three. Although I use water-based products almost exclusively, this was one occasion where time and circumstances meant I had to seek another alternative.

The second example of where water-based finishes may not be appropriate involves refinishing and restoring old furniture and antiques. Until recently, commercial furniture manufacturers did not use water-based products and certainly no antique furniture was finished with them. In all likelihood, an old piece of furniture was finished with some type of varnish, lacquer, or shellac. Trying to make a repair or do touch-up work with water-based finishes would not only look odd but also might not adhere properly. For this reason, most furniture restoration specialists avoid water-based products.

Finally, a customer may dictate when I choose not to use water-based products. In most cases, my customers don't care what material I use, as long as the finish looks good. However, occasionally a particular person may demand that the finish have the exact look or feel of another piece that was finished with lacquer. Although many water-based products have been improved to where they closely resemble traditional lacquer finishes, there are still some differences. To put it simply, water-based products are not the same as nitrocellulose lacquer, so if a customer wants a lacquer finish, that is what I give them.

2

What Are Water-Based Finishes?

Until I started using water-based finishes, I had little interest in what a finish was made of or how it worked. All I really cared about was how easy it was to apply and how consistently I could get good results. Once I started spraying water-based lacquer, all that changed. These finishes were quite different from the oils and varnishes I was used to. Applying them was often a nightmare, and I found that when I turned to other people for help I was usually met with a blank stare. I was even surprised that the customer service departments of the manufacturers whose products I was using often had little or no knowledge of how they worked. I quickly realized that if I wanted to get good, consistent results with these finishes, regardless of the application methods or conditions, I would have to first understand how they worked. This meant not only learning about water-based products but all finishes in general. Since my chemistry

experience was limited to one year in high school, I had to start from scratch. There is no doubt that understanding how all finishes work has helped me learn how to apply them.

In this chapter, I'll take a look at what water-based finishes are and how they work. I will also explain some of the terminology used when discussing these finishes so you can better understand what they are and how to use them.

Types of wood finishes

Finishes can be classified according to how they penetrate the surface of the wood and how they cure. In general terms, a wood finish is a liquid that dries to form a protective barrier over the surface being finished. Basically, all finishes consist of two elements: resins, which are the solids that dry to form the finish, and the solvents, which are the

Common penetrating finishes include natural oils like tung and walnut, as well as oils that have added driers and hardeners like the Danish oil on the left.

vehicles that carry the resin. However, finish technology is not quite that simple. While some finishes may contain only these two ingredients, others may contain 5, 10, or even 20 different substances. Furthermore, not all finishes act the same when placed on a piece of wood.

The most common types of finishes used by woodworkers fall into one of three categories: those that are absorbed by the wood (penetrating), those that lie on the surface of the wood (surface film), and those that do a little of both (penetrating film).

In some sense, all finishes dry through a process of evaporation. The vehicle that carries the resins, usually called the solvent, evaporates from the surface of the wood, leaving the resin behind to dry to a hard film. However, how those resins form the final finish varies, so all finishes can be further classified into one of three categories, according to how they cure: evaporative, reactive, and coalescing.

PENETRATING FINISHES

Penetrating finishes are those that are absorbed into the pores of the wood. Oil finishes, such as tung, linseed, and Danish oil, are all examples of penetrating finishes. Since these finishes actually become part of the wood, they are easy to apply and require no special equipment. All that is needed is a clean rag to wipe on and buff off multiple coats. However, they offer relatively little protection from water, chemicals, and general abuse. Fortunately, since the oil penetrates the surface of the wood, new coats can be applied any time, so repairing damage is fairly easy.

SURFACE FILM FINISHES

As the name implies, surface film finishes are those that do not penetrate the wood but dry to a film on its surface. Wax and water-based products are finishes that lie on the surface of the wood. Film finishes offer better resistance to moisture, stains, and scratches than penetrating products, but

Wax and water-based finishes form films that lie on the surface of the wood.

they often lack the color associated with oil finishes. Repairing film finishes requires more work than a penetrating finish, and adhesion of one coat to another may be an issue.

PENETRATING FILM FINISHES

As the name implies, these finishes not only form a film on the surface of the wood but also penetrate the pores. Both nitrocellulose lacquer and oil-based varnishes and polyurethanes are examples of penetrating film finishes. Their film-forming properties make them relatively tough and durable, while their penetrating qualities lend them a sense of warmth and depth. In short, these finishes offer the best of both worlds and have been the choice of professional woodworkers and large furniture companies for years.

EVAPORATIVE FINISHES

Evaporative finishes are probably the easiest to explain and understand. Although finishes may contain any number of additives that control color, drying time, sandability, and so on, they all contain resins, or solids, that are dissolved in a solvent. As the solvent

Traditional nitrocellulose lacquer and solvent-based varnish and polyurethane exhibit characteristics of both penetrating and film-forming finishes.

evaporates, the resins dry to form a film. The only difference between the resins before they were dissolved in the solvent and after the solvent has evaporated is their shape.

The resins used in shellac and nitrocellulose lacquer, the two most common evaporative finishes, can be

EVAPORATIVE FINISHES

Evaporative finishes cure through a process of evaporation. As the solvent leaves the finish, the resins are left behind, drying to form a continuous film.

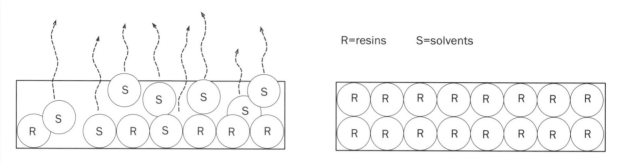

R=resins   S=solvents

ADDING AN EVAPORATIVE FINISH TO A PREVIOUS COAT

The solvent in an evaporative finish will dissolve, or melt, previous layers, so the resulting film is one continuous coat.

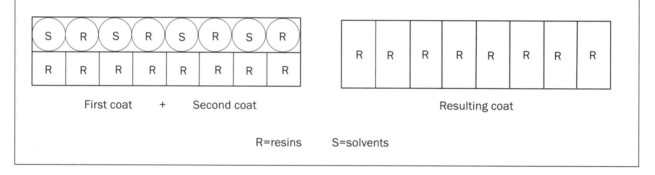

First coat   +   Second coat

Resulting coat

R=resins   S=solvents

redissolved at any time by simply pouring solvent on the dried film. This property, often referred to as "burning in" or "melting in," means shellac and lacquer are very forgiving, easy-to-use finishes. If you don't like the results, simply apply more finish. Unless a contaminant like dust is trapped in the finish, you usually don't need to sand between coats. If you do have to sand, you don't need to worry about removing the sanding dust—it will simply get redissolved by the next coat and become part of the finish.

Another nice property of evaporative finishes like shellac and lacquer is that because each application reactivates the existing film, adhesion between coats is never a problem. In fact, as one coat is applied over another, it partially liquefies the first coat and the two flow together to form one homogenous film.

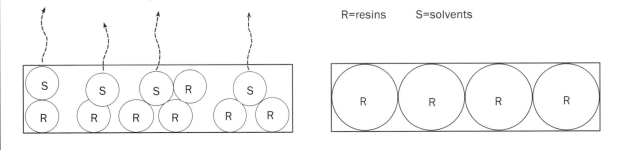

Reactive finishes are those where the resins undergo a chemical change as the solvents evaporate. The resins crosslink to form new, larger molecules.

R=resins   S=solvents

REACTIVE FINISHES

Like evaporative finishes, reactive finishes may contain several additives such as solvents, pigments, binders, and retarders. The difference is in the types of resins used to form the final film. As the various products evaporate from the finish, the resins undergo a chemical change that causes them to bond into larger molecules. This process, usually referred to as "crosslinking" or "polymerization," can be triggered by the resins reacting with oxygen or through the introduction of an acid-based catalyst. Varnish, tung oil, and linseed oil are all examples of oxygen-curing finishes. Conversion varnish and precatalyzed lacquer are examples of finishes that need a catalyst to trigger the curing process.

The main difference between reactive and evaporative finishes is that when a reactive finish is cured, the solvent in the finish won't redissolve the film. This means that if you wait too long to apply one coat on top of another, the second coat goes on as a separate layer, sitting on top of the previous coat. For this

If a can of reactive finish, such as this pigmented primer, is left unsealed, the top will skin over fairly quickly.

reason, adhesion of one coat to another may be more of an issue. A fully cured coat must therefore be sanded, or "etched," to be sure a new coat bonds properly. Also, the dust generated from sanding will not redissolve in the next coat, so any dust left behind will become trapped in the next layer, creating a rough or bumpy surface.

ADDING A REACTIVE FINISH TO A PREVIOUS COAT

To ensure that a new coat of reactive finish bonds to a previous layer, the surface should be sanded, or etched, so the next coat has something to grab onto.

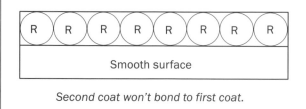

Smooth surface

Second coat won't bond to first coat.

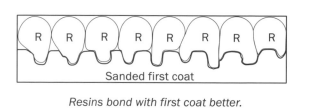

Sanded first coat

Resins bond with first coat better.

R=resins

COALESCING FINISHES

As the solvent in water-based finishes evaporates, co-solvents are left behind. These co-solvents soften the resin particles, which in turn bond together, or coalesce, to form the final film.

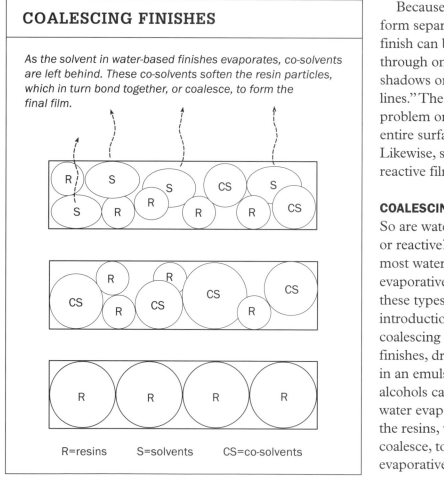

R=resins   S=solvents   CS=co-solvents

Because reactive film finishes may form separate layers, rubbing out the finish can be more difficult. If you rub through one layer, you may develop shadows or rings known as "witness lines." The only way to correct this problem once it occurs is to sand the entire surface and apply another coat. Likewise, spot repairs and touch-ups of reactive film finishes can be a bit tricky.

COALESCING FINISHES

So are water-based finishes evaporative or reactive? The simple answer is that most water-based products are evaporative. However, to better describe these types of finishes means the introduction of a third category—coalescing finishes. In water-based finishes, droplets of resin are suspended in an emulsion of water and slow-drying alcohols called glycol ethers. As the water evaporates, the glycol ethers soften the resins, which then fuse together, or coalesce, to form the dry film. Like evaporative finishes, coalescing finishes

Comparison of Finishes

Type of finish	Surface penetration	Curing method
Water-based products	Surface film	Coalescing
Shellac	Penetrating film	Evaporative
Nitrocellulose lacquer	Penetrating film	Evaporative
Oil-based varnish/polyurethane	Penetrating film	Reactive
Conversion varnishes	Surface film	Reactive
Tung, linseed oil	Penetrating	Reactive

cure through the evaporation of the solvent. The resins then link together to form the finish film.

How water-based finishes work

In general terms, water-based finishes are no different from their solvent-based counterparts. They consist of resins, or solids, and a vehicle to carry the resins in liquid form. However, water-based products are more complicated than this because the carrier, which is water, is not compatible with the resins. As a result, the two must be forced to exist together in what is known as an emulsion. This is done by adding products known as "surfactants" that help keep the resins in solution. In addition to the resins, carrier (water), and surfactants, water-based products contain numerous products that help flow and leveling, control drying, and reduce foaming. The types and amounts of these additives vary from one manufacturer to the next.

While there may be as many as 20 different chemicals in a water-based finish, the resins, water, and surfactants are the keys to how these finishes work.

RESINS
The most important part of any finish is the resin used to form the final film, and this is especially true with water-based products. The type and quality of the resin or resins contained in the emulsion have a direct effect on the performance and appearance of the dry finish. The current generation of water-based products consist, for the most part, of one of three types of plastic resins: acrylic, urethane, and an acrylic/urethane mix.

Acrylics Acrylic resins can best be described as clear plastic similar to Plexiglas. They are flexible but not very abrasion resistant. Water-based products made with acrylic resins offer relatively poor resistance to chemicals. Also, acrylic resins are clear and impart little or no color to the underlying wood.

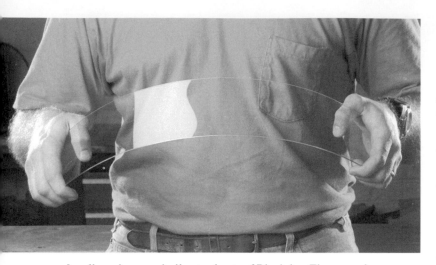

Acrylic resins are similar to sheets of Plexiglas. They are clear yet flexible.

While this may be a disadvantage if you are trying to achieve a warm, amber glow to your finish, it does come in handy when working with light-colored woods or pickled finishes.

Acrylic resins are the least expensive of the three resin types, so finishes made solely with acrylics tend to cost less than products containing urethane. Acrylics have very good bonding properties and will stick to just about anything, which helps eliminate adhesion problems between coats of dissimilar materials.

Urethane While urethane resins are also a type of plastic, they are much tougher than acrylics. Water-based finishes containing pure urethane resins are extremely scratch resistant. For this reason, finishes made with urethane are generally used on high-traffic areas like floors. Unfortunately, urethane resins are costly to produce, so finishes made with them are on the high end of the price scale. For example, a good-quality water-based floor finish suitable for a bowling alley or gym floor may cost upwards of $75 per gallon.

Acrylic/urethane blends Many of the water-based finishes on the market today consist of a mixture of acrylic and urethane resins. The acrylics keep the finish clear and inexpensive, while the urethanes add toughness and resistance to scratching and chemicals. The properties, and cost, of the finish depend on the percentage of acrylic and urethane resins present in the mix.

The overall performance of a water-based finish not only depends on the type of resins used but also on the quality of those resins. While there are a limited number of resin manufacturers in the United States today, the products they make vary in quality and price. It follows that the best resins will be the most expensive. Less expensive resins may not offer the same protection as more expensive products—they may be more difficult to apply, may not flow out and level as well, and may be harder to rub out when dry. Also, they can be a bit cloudier in appearance than their more expensive counterparts.

WATER

As with all film-forming finishes, the resin must be suspended in a liquid vehicle, usually referred to as the carrier. In water-based products, the carrier is, obviously, water. The main concern is how much and what type of water the finishes contain. The chemical composition and pH of the water used in these finishes plays an important role in how they perform. Deionized water is normally used in an effort to limit the

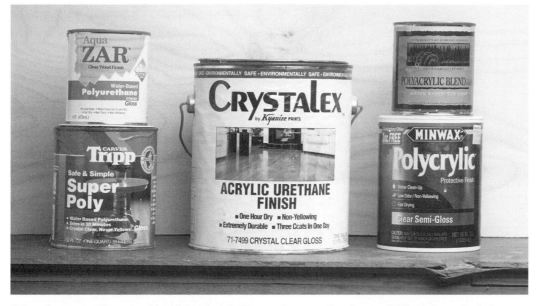

Often the name of a water-based product indicates the type of resins used. The two on the left are made with urethanes, while the three on the right contain both acrylic and urethane resins.

disruption of the various chemicals in the formula. The water should ideally have a pH of around 8 to 8.5. Water that is too low or too high in pH may disrupt the stability of the resins and may cause the grain of the wood to raise considerably.

CO-SOLVENTS

In simple terms, co-solvents are the solvents used in water-based products to soften the resins and allow them to stick together. The most common chemicals used as co-solvents are alcohols called glycol ether. Glycol ethers, which you may recognize by the trade name Butyl Cellosolve, are very slow-drying alcohols that are totally miscible (or capable of being mixed) with water. As the water evaporates, the slower-drying glycol ether is left behind to soften the resins so they can coalesce. The amount of co-solvents used in the mix is critical. If

not enough are added, the film will not form properly. On the other hand, too great an amount of co-solvents not only increases the amount of environmentally hazardous pollutants in the finish but also slows down the drying time.

Co-solvents also play a critical role in how one coat bonds to another. While a water-based finish will not completely burn in to a previous coat, the co-solvents in the finish will soften a dried coat enough so a subsequent application melts in to a degree.

The exact amount that one coat melts in to another is a subject of much misinformation and disagreement. Some manufacturers claim their products achieve 100% burn in, while others say the level is closer to 25%. It has been my experience that most of the newer generation of water-based finishes melt in and bond to previous coats to some degree but certainly not to the extent of

The surface tension of water is high, which explains why it tends to bead up rather than flow out smoothly.

shellac or lacquer. This partial melting in means the coats bond to each other and to solvent-based finishes much better than they did in the past. However, since the coats do not completely melt in, rubbing out these finishes can still lead to the creation of witness lines.

TAIL SOLVENTS

In addition to co-solvents, water-based products contain other extremely slow-drying alcohols that are usually referred to as tail solvents. Tail solvents are additives that remain with a coating for a relatively long time in its applied state. They are used to improve flow and leveling and help in maintaining a wet edge during applications. Tail solvents reduce or eliminate problems like orange peel and dimpling and are the last chemicals to evaporate from the finish as it cures.

SURFACTANTS

Surfactants, another class of additives, have an effect on how water-based products flow out. Water has a relatively high surface tension and, if not treated properly, would not flow over the surface of the wood very well. (Think about how water beads up when splashed on a finished surface.) Surfactants, which are generally petroleum-based products, are added to the finish to reduce surface tension, thus helping to improve a product's ability to flow and level smoothly.

Surfactants also play a critical role in keeping the resins suspended in the water. As mentioned, the resins used in water-based products are not compatible with water. If left to their own devices, the two simply will not mix. Keeping the resins in solution requires the addition of these surfactants, which act as a bridge between the resins and the water. The resulting liquid is known as an emulsion.

DEFOAMERS

Defoamers do exactly what their name says: They reduce the amount of foam in a finish. The surface tension of the water in the finish is reduced by surfactants, however, this lowering of the surface tension means that bubbles will form in the finish quite easily. These bubbles fall into two categories: micro, which are tiny, almost invisible bubbles that become trapped inside a finish as it cures (particularly when spraying), and macro, which are large bubbles kicked up by shaking or overbrushing a finish. Microbubbles can render a finish cloudy or hazy and can dull a gloss shine, while macrobubbles leave a finish looking and feeling rough and bumpy. Defoamers, which are primarily silicone-based products, reduce foaming and bubbling by acting to break the bubbles as soon as they form. The bubbles still exist; they just don't last for more than a split second.

MIXING IT ALL TOGETHER

Today's water-based finishes contain varying types and amounts of each of the products just listed, along with numerous other additives. In fact, a water-based coating may have leveling agents, wetting agents, fungicides, mildicides, pigments, soaps, hardeners, thickeners, and binders, to name just a few. The beauty of these products is that manufacturers can control just about any aspect of the finish, such as sandability, drying time, scuff resistance, and color, by the quality of the products they use and how they mix them. The trick is to find the right combination of materials to create a finish with as many desirable qualities as possible. While one finish may flow and level nicely, its color may be poor. Or another may dry quickly but offer poor resistance to scratches or chemicals. Still another may have good color but poor rubbing qualities.

Since the manufacturers of these products guard their formulations very closely, there is no easy way to know just how much of what type of resins, co-solvents, and other additives are used in a product. The best way I know to determine if a finish is right for your project is to try it on a sample piece of wood and see how it holds up under varying conditions.

Shaking a water-based product is one of the worst things you can do. The bubbles formed will become trapped in the finish, making it feel rough or lumpy. Always stir these products slowly and gently.

Is it water based or water borne?

Perhaps the biggest confusion surrounding water-based products is what to call them. There seem to be almost as many different names for these finishes as there are products on the market. Over the last few years, I have seen them referred to as water based, water borne, water reducible, aqueous, and latex. Furthermore, some people call them water-*base* finishes, while others refer to them as water-*based* finishes. For all practical purposes, the products on the market today that have some amount of water in them can be called whatever you, or their manufacturers, want. For the sake of simplicity, I have been referring to everything in this book as water-based finishes, but I could just as easily have picked latex or water-borne finishes.

Material Safety Data Sheets

Usually a coating will have a list of its major ingredients on the label, so determining what it is or how it is made is fairly easy. In general, if the cleanup instructions say to use water, it is a water-based product. But most finish manufacturers guard their water-based recipes very carefully, and the label may offer little help when trying to determine the type of resins used or what some of the other additives may be. If you wish to learn more about a particular finish, the best thing to do is contact the manufacturer or supplier and request a Material Safety Data Sheet (MSDS).

An MSDS is a detailed description of a product that the Federal Government requires all manufacturers to provide. A typical MSDS lists the main ingredients in a product and whether they are toxic. For finishes, an MSDS also lists things like the flash point of the material (the temperature at which it will ignite) and any special precautions that must be taken when storing, handling, or applying the product. An MSDS also lists potential health hazards, first-aid advice, any special clothing needed, and fire precautions that must be taken.

Professional woodshops are required to maintain a file of MSDSs on all liquids and chemicals they use. If you want to know more about a finish you are using, don't hesitate to call the manufacturer and request an MSDS.

Information Included on a Material Safety Data Sheet

Manufacturer

Address

Telephone Number

I. Product Identification
- Trade name
- Color index name
- Chemical family
- Chemical formula
- TSCA status
- RTECS no.

II. Hazardous Ingredients
- Components

III. Physical Data
- Appearance & odor
- Solubility in water

IV. Fire & Explosion Data
- Flash point
- Extinguishing media
- Special procedures for fighting fire
- Usual hazards

V. Health Hazard Effects Data
- Animal toxicity
- Oral
- Eye effects
- Skin effects
- Human effects

VI. Emergency First-Aid Procedures
- Inhalation
- Ingestion
- Eye contact
- Skin contact

VII. Reactivity Data
- Stability
- Conditions to avoid
- Polymerization
- Incompatible materials
- Hazardous decomposition products

VIII. Precautions for Safe Handling, Use, and Disposal
- Steps to be taken in case material is released or spilled
- Waste disposal

IX. Special Protection Information
- Respiratory protection
- Ventilation
- Protective gloves
- Eye protection
- Other

X. Special Precaution

XI. Shipping Data

XII. HMIS Rating

Some manufacturers call their products water based, while others are water borne or water reducible.

People who work in the chemical coatings industry do make a distinction between water based and water borne, but, to add to the confusion, they do not always agree on the exact definition of these two terms. Some manufacturers are vague, while others attempt to quantify their definitions with numbers. The consensus is that water-based products are just that: finishes that contain water as the primary *solvent*. Water-borne products, on the other hand, are defined as solvent-based materials that have been tweaked, through the addition of various chemicals, to accept water into the emulsion as a *carrier*. In this sense, water-reducible products are similar to water-borne finishes in that they are not truly based on using water as the main solvent but have been adjusted to accept water as a thinning agent.

Some manufacturers are more specific in how they distinguish between water-based and water-borne finishes. For example, one chemist considers any product that contains 50% or more water to be truly water based, while any finish that contains less than 50% water is simply a solvent finish that has been redesigned to accept water as a reducing agent.

Perhaps as these finishes continue to develop and become more readily available and accepted by the woodworking industry a naming convention will be adopted that is consistent and understood by all. Until then, I think that for most people it is irrelevant whether something is called water based, water borne, or water reducible, since all these terms refer to a class of finishes that use water to some degree as the solvent, or carrier, and cleaning agent.

3

Development of Water-Based Finishes

Not too long ago, I gave a talk on water-based finishes to an amateur woodworkers' club. The first thing I did was ask how many people had used water-based finishes at least once. Of the 40 people present, about five raised their hands. Next, I asked how many of them has used latex paint. Not suprisingly, all 40 people raised their hands. Most of them realized right away that I had asked them a trick question, for, after all, latex paint is a water-based finish. In fact, it was the first water-based finish ever developed for commercial use. What we now think of as water-based finishes were developed several years after the introduction of latex paint and weren't readily available commercially until the early 1980s.

Early alternatives to oil-based finishes

During World War II, petroleum products, which are used extensively in oil-based paints and finishes, were being diverted to the war effort. As a result, paint manufacturers began looking for alternatives to traditional solvent-based paints. They needed something that was durable, easy to apply, and had the look and feel of oil paint but used less petroleum products. Their first attempts consisted of taking an oil-based paint and reformulating it by replacing the linseed, tung, or cotton oil resins with latex, a material pulled from the rubber tree. They then removed some of the petroleum-based solvents by thinning the formulation with water. Unfortunately this did not work very well. The products performed poorly, were

Most woodworkers are already familiar with water-based products in the form of latex paint.

difficult to apply, and ironically could not be cleaned up with water. In short, they proved to be an inadequate replacement for traditional oil-based paints.

After the war, there was a tremendous need for new housing. Because of this building boom, flooring manufacturers began searching for stronger, harder forms of prefabricated floor coverings. Polyurethane, a resin developed in the 1930s to harden airplane tires, proved to be just what the flooring industry was looking for. These resins were extremely hard, durable, and resisted scratching and most household chemicals.

As plastic resin technology improved during the 1950s, polyurethanes and acrylics began to be incorporated into clear wood finishes. These tough coatings were the perfect finish for high-traffic areas like bowling alleys and gymnasium floors, but they had their problems. The petroleum-based products were toxic, smelly, and extremely flammable. Being responsible for burning down a building was not an

The resins commonly found in today's water-based finishes were originally developed for the prefabricated-flooring industry.

attractive prospect to professional floor finishers. They needed something that was safe to use and dried fast. This demand played a great part in fueling the development of water-based finishes as we know them today.

Government pressure for environmentally safe products

By the late 1970s, the technology for creating water-based finishes was in place. However, outside of the flooring industry, no one really had an interest in these new products. Furniture manufacturers had been using the same solvent-based materials with great success for years, so why would they want to switch to a new product that looked and acted differently?

All that began to change in the early 1980s. As air quality became more of an issue, government bodies began to regulate the amount of pollutants large companies were allowed to emit into the atmosphere. Probably the most well-known regulatory agency is located in Southern California. The South Coast Air Quality Management District (SCAQMD) took a hard look at the quality of air in that region and set limits on the amount of VOCs that large companies could emit.

At first there was great resistance among industry to making any changes. However, as both government and public pressures increased, large users of pollution-causing materials realized that eventually they would have to find ways to comply to VOC-emission limits. The first thing large furniture manufacturers did was look at their application methods and equipment. They quickly concluded that the easiest way to lower VOC emissions was to reduce the amount of finish being used. As a result, finishing technology, which remained relatively unchanged since the development of compressed-air spray guns, began to improve dramatically. Airless, electrostatic, and HVLP systems all began to be used as manufacturers scrambled to comply with new, stricter rules.

The SCAQMD's finishing rules were drafted in 1983 and scheduled to take effect in 1988. However, many large woodworking companies successfully argued that the technology available in 1988 was not sufficient to allow them to comply with the rules without greatly decreasing the quality of their finished products. As a result, the deadline for compliance was postponed until 2005, with an interim rule taking effect on July 1, 1997. This interim rule, #1136, set separate standards for various types of finishes, including stains, sealers, and clear and pigmented topcoats.

The goal of the interim rule is to reduce the amount of VOCs emitted into Southern California's air by about 45%, or 5 tons per day. To do this, the rule establishes limits on the amount of VOCs various types of finishes can have.

One way large furniture manufacturers have reduced emissions of VOCs is by switching from older compressed air guns, like the one on the right, to newer, more efficient HVLP systems, like the one on the left.

VOCs and HAPs

When talking about finishes and air quality, the terms volatile organic compounds (VOCs) and hazardous air pollutants (HAPs) are used to describe the various chemicals that are emitted into the air as finishes dry. What, if any, difference is there between a VOC and an HAP? That's a good question that could lead to a textbook-like discussion of chemicals and how they affect the atmosphere but I'll try to keep it simple.

VOCs are the solvents that evaporate from a finish, leaving behind the nonvolatile solids. VOCs are generally described as hydrocarbon compounds that react with sunlight to form smog. The level of VOCs in a finish are of great concern to various government agencies, which have begun to be strictly regulate VOC emissions. By limiting the amount of VOCs contained in finishing products, agencies like California's South Coast Air Quality Management District hope to significantly improve air quality.

With the passage of the Clean Air Act in the late 1980s, a new class of substances, HAPs, was introduced. Like VOCs, HAPs are the chemicals that evaporate from drying finishes and cause air pollution.

What makes a chemical an HAP or a VOC can be a bit confusing. In simple terms, HAPs are a type of product, while VOCs are numerical measurements of hazardous emissions. A solvent itself is not a VOC, but it may release VOCs into the atmosphere. For the average woodworker, understanding the technical differences between VOCs and HAPs may not be that important. However, the fact that they are beginning to be regulated does have a direct impact on anyone who uses water-based finishes. As the types and amounts of HAPs and VOCs that can be contained in a finish are regulated and reduced, wood finishers will continue to see improvements in low-VOC coatings and will have a bigger and better selection of water-based finishes in the future.

Although this rule sets strict limits for total VOC output, it does allow for some flexibility as to how manufacturers meet these limits. For example, a company could lower the VOC amount in both a sealer and a topcoat, or it could keep the amount in the sealer the same and reduce the topcoat even more. When the full rule takes effect in 2005, the amount of VOCs in all types of finishes will have to be reduced to even lower levels.

While manufacturers have been able to significantly reduce the amount of VOC emissions by changing finishing and filtration systems, many of them will probably begin switching to at least some water-based products to comply with the 2005 limits.

Although SCAQMD's rule 1136 only applies to Southern California, its impact on the rest of the country has been profound. In fact, the Clean Air Act passed by Congress defines another category of pollutants, known as HAPs (hazardous air pollutants), and limits their emission throughout the United States. Other areas of the country that have concentrated populations and manufacturing, such as the northeastern corridor from Maine to North Carolina,

So-called "clean air" finishes were probably the first low-VOC products many woodworkers became familiar with. Although these are still solvent-based materials, the amount of pollutants, or VOCs, has been greatly reduced.

Act are indirectly having a profound impact on small users and will continue to do so in the future.

As we all know, business is fueled by supply and demand. As large furniture manufacturers look for ways to comply with new rules, chemical coatings companies will put more money and effort into developing and manufacturing low-VOC coatings, including water-based finishes. It should come as no surprise that finish manufacturers will work to satisfy their large customers, often at the expense of the small consumer. As a result, the supply of traditional, high-VOC lacquers and varnishes will decrease as the demand for low-VOC coatings increases. I first began noticing this change in the early 1990s when I went into my local hardware store and discovered that they had replaced an entire group of traditional varnishes and polyurethanes with low-VOC finishes.

have been watching SCAQMD closely. Several states, like New York and New Jersey, are not far behind California in restricting the amount of VOCs and HAPs that can be emitted into the atmosphere. As a result, more and more professional woodworkers are beginning to feel that it is only a matter of time before water-based finishes are the only viable option for meeting ever-tightening rules and regulations.

So far, government regulations have only been concerned with large users and have left the small shops alone. The targets have been large companies that deal with finishes in terms of tons, rather than gallons. So, you may ask, how do these tightening regulations affect a little guy like me who only uses a few gallons per week, month, or year? Technically, at this point, they don't. However, SCAQMD's rule 1136 and the Clean Air

Advances in water-based finishes

As mentioned, water-based finishes have been around in one form or another for at least 50 years. Unfortunately, the first generation of these products left a great deal to be desired. In fact, early water-based finishes had so many problems that they quickly developed a reputation for being difficult to use. They were known to be extremely temperamental to apply and inferior in appearance and performance to typical solvent-based products. Over time, however, water-based products have improved dramatically.

PROBLEMS OF EARLY WATER-BASED FINISHES

Early water-based finishes had several problems, any one of which by itself would be a major obstacle to these finishes gaining acceptance by the general consumer. When taken as a whole, the problems associated with water-based products made them undesirable to all but the most environmentally conscious users.

Severe grain raising The first and most obvious problem with early water-based finishes was that when applied to wood, the water in the formulation raised the grain significantly. Eliminating this raised grain meant more sanding and better wood preparation. While this presented a problem for furniture makers of any level, it really created difficulties for large furniture companies that were used to doing things a certain way. Adding additional labor slows down production while increasing costs, so raised grain alone was enough to turn most furniture manufacturers away from water-based finishes.

Incompatibility with other finishes As if the grain-raising problem weren't enough, furniture makers soon discovered that these finishes did not, in most cases, adhere to the solvent-based fillers, stains, toners, and glazes they were using. In order for early water-based finishes to work, the entire finishing system either had to be water based (or at least water compatible) or required the use of sealers to bond the water-based product to solvent-based undercoats. Again, most furniture manufacturers, large and small, balked at having to rethink their entire finishing operation.

Dull, lifeless color Another problem with early water-based finishes was that the resins used were synthetic plastics, as opposed to the natural resins used in solvent-based products. As a result, early water-based finishes often gave wood a dull or colorless appearance. This came as quite a shock to furniture makers and their customers, who were used to the warm, rich, amber tones associated with traditional solvent-based lacquers and varnishes. When I look back on my first experiences with water-based finishes, I remember a customer who expressed disappointment that I hadn't used a better grade of wood. "The cherry your supplier sent you was not very good quality was it?" she asked. I didn't have the heart to tell her that it wasn't the wood but the finish. The color of the finish was so poor that it made the cherry look as though it had been bleached. In fact, the heartwood was so washed out that it looked like I had used sapwood for the entire project.

Expensive One of the biggest complaints I had when I first began using water-based finishes was their cost. In general, the better-quality water-based finishes I was buying cost anywhere from $5 to $15 more per gallon than a comparable solvent-based lacquer. I understood that because the technology used to make these finishes was relatively new and user demand was low, the price would naturally be higher. Even so, I couldn't help but feel that somehow I was being penalized for using a product that was better for me and the environment.

Poor shelf life One of the advantages of water-based finishes is they contain a high solids content, which means the finishes build fast and you get a thick dry film. However, they also contain numerous ingredients in precise amounts that must be in balance all the time. Early versions of water-based products were not very stable, and in some cases the additives coagulated as the finish grew old. This was especially bad for small shops that may not use an entire can of finish quickly. It was also hard on manufacturers and their distributors, who had to keep an eye on the age of their stock. On at least one occasion, I have opened a new 5-gallon pail of pigmented lacquer only to discover that no matter how much I stirred I could not get the solids back into solution.

PRODUCT IMPROVEMENTS

By the early 1990s, large finishing operations had a real problem on their hands. They needed to find ways to comply with ever stricter regulations but the options available were inadequate. Fortunately, increasing demand for water-based products meant coating manufacturers now had incentive to put time, effort, and money into developing a new generation of compliant finishes. As a result, the number and types of water-based finishes has exploded in the past several years to the point where just about every manufacturer of finish coatings offers at least one if not a complete line of water-based products.

Most of the water-based finishes on the market today are far superior than their older cousins. As the technology used to make these finishes has improved, the problems that made these products so unappealing in the past have gradually been reduced or overcome completely.

Because of their high solids content, water-based finishes must be stirred thoroughly before use. As they age, the solids tend to settle out of the suspension, leaving a gooey mess at the bottom of the pail.

Less raised grain As noted, one of the biggest complaints with early water-based finishes was that they raised the grain of the wood so much that finishing became a much slower and harder process. The problem was due to a number of factors, including the amount of water in the finish, the time it took for the water to evaporate, the acidity of the water, and how the finish was applied.

As the demand for better water-based products increased, finish manufacturers realized they had to reduce or, if possible, eliminate the grain-raising characteristics of these products. How they were able to do this varies from one manufacturer to the next, but improvements in resin technology combined with better-quality additives have helped create a new generation of finishes that have significantly reduced grain-raising properties. In fact, there are

Oil and water don't mix—or do they?

About six years ago, I tried putting a water-based topcoat over a solvent-based stain with disastrous results. It had taken several hours to mix a batch of stain that was a perfect match for the customer's color sample. I didn't want to use a solvent-based topcoat for fear that it would yellow or darken the stain. The can of water-based finish said it could be applied over pigmented stains that were fully dry, so I applied a fairly heavy coat of stain and let it sit overnight before brushing on the finish.

Everything seemed to be going fine until I came into the shop the next day. The clear topcoat had begun to bubble and peel, which meant the entire finish had to be stripped off. I ended up using a solvent-based finish that did indeed change the color of the piece just enough so it was no longer a perfect match,

but fortunately the customer didn't mind.

I later learned what had gone wrong. The water-based product would have worked fine over the solvent-based stain if the stain had been cured, not just dry to the touch. I later did some test pieces with the same materials and found that if I let the stain dry 48 hours, instead of just 12, the water-based finish adhered with no problems.

Fortunately, as water-based finishes have improved, their ability to adhere to solvent-based products has increased significantly. In fact, one woodworker who specializes in high-end rocking chairs regularly puts water-based topcoats over Danish oil finishes. When he first told me this I was surprised and somewhat curious as to why and how he did this. It turns out that

he uses a rubbing, or Danish, oil that is relatively fast drying. He applies one coat of oil to give the wood better color while providing the finish with a better sense of depth. After the oil has dried overnight, he applies a water-based topcoat with no adhesion problems.

If you had asked me six years ago whether water-based finishes could be used over solvent-based products, my answer would have been an emphatic no. However, water-based finishes have improved to the point where adhesion problems have been greatly reduced or even eliminated. I still think it is a good idea to let the solvent finish dry for as long as possible and recommend using sealers if you fear any possible problems, but if you ask me today whether water and oil can be mixed, I would have to say yes.

---

several products on the market today that raise the grain no more than a good coat of shellac.

Fewer compatibility problems Another benefit of the newer water-based resins and formulations is that they are more compatible with solvent-based finishes. In particular, improvements in technology have led to the development

of resins that are able to "etch" or grab hold of previously finished surfaces. A few years ago, I would have never considered putting a water-based topcoat over a solvent-based stain without some type of sealer. Today, there are many water-based products that can be used over oil finishes of all types with little or no problem.

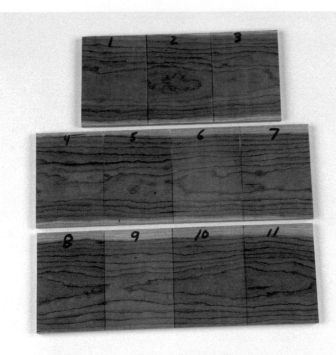

Some water-based finishes are better than others at emulating traditional lacquer. To demonstrate how these products vary in color, this cherry board was coated with the following products: 1—nitrocellulose lacquer; 2—water-based sanding sealer; 3—water-based lacquer; 4 and 5—water-based polyurethanes; 6 and 7—water-based poly/acrylic blends; 8—water-based acrylic; 9—water-based lacquer; 10—shellac; 11—water-based lacquer over shellac.

Better color Another benefit of improved resins is that the color and appearance of the finish has been greatly improved. Whereas older generation finishes often looked dull and lifeless, several of the newer products on the market more closely emulate traditional lacquers and varnishes. That is not to say that all new brands of water-based finish will give a piece of wood that desirable amber glow. The finishes are only as good as the resins used. As a result, some finishes still impart little color to the wood or appear cloudy or even bluish

when dry. The best way to check the final appearance of a finish is to test it on a piece of scrap before using it on your completed project.

Less expensive Another benefit to arise from the increasing demand for water-based products is that their price is beginning to come in line with other types of finish. While some manufacturers are still charging a premium for their water-based products, prices have been inching downward over the last few years. I currently use a water-based lacquer that costs only a few dollars per gallon more than its nitrocellulose counterpart. I suspect that as more people switch to water-based products the downward trend in prices will continue and may even accelerate.

When I look back at my first attempts to use water-based finishes I am amazed at how much improvement has been made in a relatively short period of time. In fact, the finishes I use today are so superior to those of just five years ago that it is hard to believe they are related in any way. When I recall the difficulties I had applying those older products and the number of times I had to bring things back to the shop for refinishing, I often wonder how and why I continued using water-based materials. But for numerous reasons, including lack of space, lack of funds for a spray booth, and health concerns, I made a commitment to use water-based finishes almost exclusively. I stuck with them until I had learned to overcome whatever problems arose. Fortunately for woodworkers just starting out, the newer products on the market are superior in performance and much easier to use than the older generation of finishes.

Surface Preparation

No matter what type of finish you use, the final results ultimately depend on how well you prepare the surface. This is especially true with water-based products. Although you may be able to get a good finish on an improperly prepared piece, you will spend a lot more time sanding and recoating than would otherwise be necessary. The steps involved in proper surface preparation, including sanding, prewetting the wood, and using fillers and putties, depend on several factors such as the species of wood being finished, how well the item was constructed, the type of finish materials used, and whether the finish is clear or opaque. However, no matter what type of finish you use, all surface preparation begins with sanding.

Sanding

Although hand-rubbed oil finishes look nice and are easy to apply, they do have a few drawbacks. In particular, because the oil is absorbed into the wood, minor surface defects like sanding scratches are highlighted by the finish. Most water-based products form a film that sits on the surface of the wood. This means minor imperfections can, to a degree, be hidden beneath the finish. As a result, scratches and flaws left behind after sanding may not be as noticeable.

"Great," you're probably thinking, "I don't have to do much sanding when using water-based products!" To a certain extent this is true. Because water-based products sit on the surface of the wood, the finish tends to bond better to a

The scratch on this piece of cherry is plainly visible under the oil finish on the top but is much harder to see when coated with the water-based finish on the bottom.

rough surface than to a surface that has been polished with a high-grit sandpaper. When working with Danish oil finishes, I regularly sand a piece to at least 180 grit and often 220 grit or higher. With water-based finishes, I rarely sand beyond 120 grit and I never go higher than 180 grit before applying the first coat of finish.

Although you may not have to spend a great deal of time sanding a piece prior to finishing, it does not mean you can be careless or do a sloppy job. After all, the better the surface is prepared the better the finish will be. While a few tiny marks and blemishes may not be as much of a problem as they would with wiped-on oil, you obviously want to minimize surface defects as much as possible.

Another reason for careful sanding when using water-based products is related to grain raising. The water in these finishes swells wood fibers, causing them to stand up. While the amount of grain raised depends in great part on the brand or type of finish being used,

sanding also plays an important role in how much grain is raised by the first coat. The more carefully you sand a piece prior to finishing, the less the grain will raise.

While there are a few general guidelines as to the grits and techniques used in sanding, the actual sanding equipment and grits used is largely a matter of personal preference. Begin with the lowest grit needed to remove large surface defects and scratches, then progress to the next higher grit. When using power sanders, I like to start with relatively big machines, decreasing the size and weight of the sander as the grit increases. For example, when sanding a door panel, I may use a heavy industrial belt sander with a 60-grit or 80-grit belt to flatten the surface and remove any noticeable defects like dings and glue spots. Next, I place the next highest grit on the sander and further smooth the surface by removing all of the scratch marks left by the previous belt.

When choosing sanding equipment, begin with heavy, aggressive machines and work your way to smaller, lighter sanders.

After flattening the piece with a belt sander, I switch to a finer grit and a smaller, lighter machine. If the surface is large, like a tabletop, I use a 6-in.-diameter random-orbit sander. If the piccc is smaller or contains a lot of tight areas, I use a palm sander. These lighter machines remove the parallel scratches left behind by the belt sander, replacing them with a set of random scratches that are finer and harder to see. I often use the same grit on the random-orbit sander as I just used on the belt sander and then follow up with a final light sanding with the next highest grit.

If I am planning to use a pigmented stain as my first coat of finish, I may sand the piece up to 180 grit to ensure there are no large scratches for the pigment to become lodged in. However, when working with water-based finishes, I generally sand the wood to 120 grit or 150 grit to ensure the first coat of finish has a good surface to bite into.

Proper grit selection plays a direct role in not only how fast you sand a piece but also in how much effort the sanding takes. The main thing to remember when selecting sandpaper is that the next grit in your sanding sequence should remove all of the scratches left by the previous grit while leaving its own set of smaller, finer scratches. It is important that the scratch pattern is even and consistent, especially if you plan to use a pigmented stain. A board sanded with a relatively low grit that has a consistent scratch pattern parallel with the grain and doesn't contain any unusually deep or wide scratches will be easier to finish and will ultimately look better than a board that is sanded with a finer grit but is uneven and contains scratches that vary in size.

Prewetting

If I am looking for an exceptionally fine finish on a piece or if I want to minimize the amount of grain raised by the first coat of finish, I may prewet the surface before applying the seal coat. Simply, this involves wetting the wood, letting it dry, then sanding it. The water raises the grain just as the water in the first coat of finish would, then after the wood has dried, the stiffened fibers are sanded off.

I use a spray bottle to apply a light mist on the wood, but you could also use a rag or sponge. The key is to get the surface of the wood damp, not to soak it throughout. Don't worry if you get a little too much water on the wood—you can always wipe it off with a rag. Although you would practically have to use a garden hose or dunk the wood in a bucket of water to cause any real harm, it makes sense to use as little water as possible.

After spraying or wiping on a light coat of water, let the wood sit until dry. On a warm, dry day, wood that has been given a light misting may be ready to sand in 15 or 20 minutes. If the application of water is heavier or if the weather is cold or humid, the piece may need to dry for an hour or two. Some recommend that the wood dry overnight before sanding. In theory this is fine, but the reality of tight schedules often means I must sand the dampened wood as soon as possible. While I prefer to wait a few hours, I have regularly sanded things after only a few minutes of drying time. The bottom line is if the wood looks and feels dry, chances are it is dry. You'll know the wood is dry if the fibers are easy to sand and turn to dust quickly. If the fibers are soft and don't sand easily or if the sandpaper gums up, then the wood is still too wet to sand.

Because you are only trying to remove the raised grain and not alter the scratch pattern in the wood, you can skip several grits from where you finished dry sanding. For example, if I dry sanded to 120 grit, I may use 180 grit to smooth the raised grain. However, I never wet sand above 220 grit, since anything finer will not do a good job of removing the stiffened fibers.

The type of paper used when wet sanding is really a matter of personal preference. I like to use a silicon carbide paper that is designed for both wet and dry sanding. Often called wet/dry or auto paper, it is easily recognized by its evenly sized grit and black color.

It doesn't matter whether you wet the wood with a spray bottle, rag, or sponge before sanding. The idea is not to soak the surface but to merely dampen it.

Wet/dry sandpapers are usually black, while stearated papers may be white or pink.

Although stearated papers work well for sanding off raised grain, I generally avoid them. Stearates are soaps designed to lubricate the paper to make it easier to use. Unfortunately, these soaps have a tendency to clump and form little specks. Any stearates left behind on the surface of the wood will show through the finish as a small spot or depression called fisheye.

If you do use stearated papers, it is important to remove all of the sanding dust with a damp cloth prior to finishing. I prefer to dampen the cloth with water, but if you are concerned about contaminants on the surface of the finish you could moisten the cloth with mineral spirits. If you use mineral spirits, be sure to use very small amounts. A puddle of mineral spirits left sitting on the surface may soften the finish. Above all, never use steel wool at this stage in

the finishing process. Small particles may become lodged in the pores of the wood and will show up well after the finish has dried as little black specks of rust.

Using paste fillers

In some cases, the final finish you are trying to create may only be achieved by first filling the pores of the wood. This is especially true when working with open-grained woods like oak, mahogany, ash, and walnut. Although there will be times when you want to maintain that open-grained look, there will be other instances when you want the finished surface to be as smooth as possible. Using paste fillers on your project not only helps to create a surface that is like

The oil-based paste filler on the left and the water-based product on the right look alike in texture and work the same. Other than the color, only real differences are how fast they dry and how compatible they are with other finishes.

glass but also allows you to introduce another element of color into the final finish.

When discussing paste, or pore, fillers, it is important to note the distinction between a wood filler and a wood putty. Fillers are used to fill the open pores on the surface of the wood. They are used to give the wood a smooth, glassy surface and can also be used to impart interesting colors and contrasts in the appearance of the wood. Putties, on the other hand, are used to fill cracks, nail holes, gaps, and other defects.

Similarly, fillers should not be confused with sealers. Sealers are clear liquids that contain many of the same properties as a film-forming finish. Sealers do just what their name implies—they seal the surface of the wood. They can either help to seal finishes like stains and dyes in the wood or to prevent more finish from penetrating the wood. (For more on sealers, see Chapter 5.)

Paste fillers, which can be oil or water based, are thick mixtures of ground-up minerals, usually quartz or silica (referred to as silex), and solvent. Resins are also added to act as binders. Some fillers are very thick and must be thinned prior to use, while others come prethinned and can be used straight from the can. Fillers come in a variety of colors, including neutral, which can be tinted to create just about any shade imaginable.

Other than the type of solvent used, there is very little difference between an oil- and a water-based paste filler. However, there are several reasons why I choose water-based fillers whenever possible. I like them better than oil-based products because they dry faster and are easier to clean up. In addition, water-based fillers are compatible with just about any type of stain, dye, and topcoat. You can use a water-based paste filler under shellac, lacquer, varnish, and water-based finishes. Plus, unlike oil-based fillers, water-based fillers can be stained after application.

Oil-based paste fillers may not be a good choice when working with water-based topcoats. Although the newest generation of water-based products don't exhibit many of the adhesion problems associated with their predecessors, using them over oil-based fillers is still risky business. Oil-based fillers dry much slower than water-based products. If you do plan on putting a water-based topcoat over an oil-based filler, be sure to let it dry thoroughly. I would wait at least two or three days and, if possible, up to a week before applying the topcoat. I would also recommend applying a coat of dewaxed shellac as a sealer to avoid any potential adhesion problems. And, as always, it never hurts to test a sample piece first before mixing these two products on a completed piece of furniture.

THINNING PASTE FILLERS

Water-based paste fillers are designed to be used straight from the can with no thinning necessary. However, because they dry so fast, you may want to thin them a bit to give yourself a little more working time. You can use plain tap water or glycol ether as the thinner. Although glycol ether, which should be available from the manufacturer of the filler, will slow down the drying time much more than water, the filler will still dry much more quickly than an oil-based product. Even if you thin the mixture, you will have to work fast.

If you plan to use an entire can of filler at one time, you can thin it right in the container. However, if you only need a small amount, it is best to work from a separate jar or cup. This will keep dried filler from gathering on the rim of the can, making it hard to close.

For thinning, I have never noticed any difference between using warm or cold water, although warm water will be slightly easier to stir into the filler. The main thing to keep in mind is the filler should be the consistency of cream. If it is too thick, it will be hard to work, may dry too fast, and won't fill small pores very well. If it is too thin, it will be easier to apply and take a bit longer to dry, but it won't fill large pores as well. Always add small amounts of thinner to the

filler, stirring it thoroughly after the liquid is added. It is easier to make a thick filler thinner than it is to thicken a filler that has too much liquid in it.

TINTING PASTE FILLERS

The color of paste filler you choose for your project depends on your own tastes and the look you are trying to create. You can use a filler that matches the color of the wood, which will make the grain unobtrusive, or you can opt for a shade that creates striking color contrasts.

If you can't find the exact color you want, you can mix your own. Begin by purchasing the right base color. I use neutral or natural if I want to mix an earth-tone color that resembles a stain or dye, and white or off-white if I am trying to achieve a brighter, more colorful look like a pastel or primary color.

Tinting the filler is simply a matter of adding a coloring agent to the mix. When working with water-based fillers, I

Universal tints are the same colorants used by your local paint store to mix custom paints. You can buy them in small tubes and quarts.

A little tint goes a long way. The small drop shown here is enough to turn this wood putty a deep, red, earthy color.

The wood must be clean before applying paste fillers. Note how the pores on the left side of this board, which was blown off with compressed air, are brighter and more visible than those on the right side, which are clogged with dust.

use universal tinting colors (UTCs), which are pigments that can be mixed with just about any type of finish. UTCs are readily available at paint or art supply stores. A little drop of these tints

goes a long way, so I usually buy them in small, 1-ounce tubes. However, if you do a lot of finishing and use the same color tints on a regular basis, it may pay to buy larger containers. Water-based fillers can also be tinted with dry fresco powders, but these are a bit more difficult to find. Both UTCs and fresco powders work equally well, so what you use is strictly a matter of preference and availability. The main thing to remember is that the tinting agent must be a pigment. The powders used to mix dyes will do a poor job of altering the color of the filler.

Unless you plan to use an entire can of filler on one project, it is best to pour the amount needed into a separate, clean container. When adding tint to the filler, remember that UTCs are very potent and a small drop goes a long way. It is easier to add color than it is to take it away, so you should introduce the tint very carefully. Begin with a tiny drop and then, as you get a feel for how the color is developing, add small amounts until you reach the desired shade.

APPLYING PASTE FILLERS

Before you begin applying a paste filler to your project, remove all of the dust that resulted from sanding. Dust left in the pores of the wood may prevent the filler from adhering properly. In fact, you may end up removing most if not all of the filler when wiping off the excess. Since dust gets embedded deep in the pores of the wood, simply wiping the surface with a rag or brush won't do. The best way to remove all of the dust is with a blast of compressed air. If you don't own an air compressor, you can resort to the next best thing—lung power.

Once the dust is removed from your project and the filler is properly thinned and tinted, you can begin the application process. Fortunately, applying paste fillers is easy. Unfortunately, it is also messy. Begin by pouring or scooping a healthy dose of filler onto the surface of your project. Work the filler into the pores by rubbing it vigorously with a rag, plastic applicator or trowel, or stiff bristle brush. While you could use a good-quality brush for this process, chances are by the time you are done it won't be much good for anything else. When applying paste fillers, I use cheap, disposable brushes that I can throw out when I am done with them.

To work the filler into the wood, move the brush in diagonal or circular motions. Water-based fillers dry fast, so it is important to work with small areas at a time. Fillers won't leave lap marks, so don't worry about where you start or how much you do at one time. The important thing is to remove as much of the excess filler as soon as possible. Once you brush on the filler, you should wipe off the excess almost immediately. To do this, you can use a rubber squeegee, a plastic spatula, or a credit card, but I have found a thin ripping of wood works just as well. The wood can be cut to a point on one end, which helps in digging dried filler out of nooks, crannies, and inside corners.

After you have squeegeed off the excess filler, wipe the entire area with a burlap cloth. Burlap works well on both oil- and water-based fillers because it is rough enough to remove the filler but not so rough that it scratches the surface. Plus, as the cloth fills with dried material, you can shake it out and reuse it.

An inexpensive, disposable brush is a good tool for working paste filler around and into the surface of the wood.

Rubber squeegees, plastic credit cards, and scraps of wood can all be used to scrape away excess filler. The point on the wood comes in handy when trying to dig filler out of deep corners.

While you could use a regular cloth to wipe down a freshly filled surface, rough burlap works much better and is easier to keep clean.

PASTE FILLERS

Paste fillers shrink as they dry. Usually the first coat of sealer is enough to fill the resulting small depression. However, in deeply grained wood you may need to apply a second coat of filler.

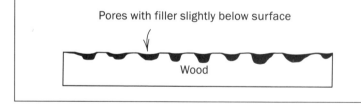

Pores with filler slightly below surface

Wood

Water-based fillers are usually dry enough to sand and topcoat in two to three hours. When sanding, the idea is to remove the filler from the surface of the wood, leaving it only in the pores. In most cases, I use 220-grit or 320-grit

wet/dry paper, but occasionally if I have applied too much filler I may have to resort to 180 grit or even 150 grit. Although I generally avoid stearated papers when working with water-based finishes, this is the one time when I may make an exception. Stearated paper makes sanding paste fillers an easier task—just be sure to remove all of the dust with a damp rag when you are done.

Paste fillers can be tricky to sand. If the filler streaks the sandpaper with a gooey substance, it is not dry. Let the filler sit until the sandpaper turns it into a light powder. Be careful how much you sand since it is easy to cut through any stain or dye that may be underneath the filler. If you applied the filler over bare wood, cutting through in a few places shouldn't pose too much of a problem. However, if the wood was stained or sealed before applying the filler, you should avoid oversanding. If you cut through a pigmented stain, you will have a tough time repairing the damage. I have found that no matter how carefully I sand paste filler, I inevitably cut through the underlying finish in at least a few sharp corners. Because of this, if the wood needs to be stained before filling, I always use water-soluble dyes. These dyes are very easy to repair when the inevitable cut-through occurs.

Paste fillers undergo a certain amount of shrinkage as they dry, so in some cases it may be necessary to apply a second coat of filler after the first coat has been sanded. This may happen if the pores of the wood are unusually large or if you didn't do a very good job of packing the filler into the pores. However, I find that in most cases the shrinkage is not significant enough to require a second application. Subsequent coats of sealer or finish are usually enough to fill any depressions left in the pores.

Once the filler has been sanded, wipe it with a slightly damp cloth to remove any residue, then buff it clean with a soft, dry cloth. At this point, the surface of the wood should appear flat and somewhat shiny. Don't worry if the surface does not feel perfectly smooth to the touch. This is usually due to a slight amount of shrinkage and will disappear with the first or second coat of sealer or finish.

I usually apply a coat of sealer between the paste filler and topcoat. The sealer not only helps to "top off" any remaining depressions in the pores but also acts as a bonding agent between the filler and the final finish coats. However, because water-based fillers bond well with water-based topcoats, a coat of sealer is not absolutely necessary and is strictly a matter of personal preference.

STAINING PASTE FILLERS

One of the nice properties of water-based fillers is that, unlike oil-based products, they can be stained after application. Any stain containing alcohol or lacquer thinner will work to color the filler. These include nongrain-raising (NGR) dyes, which are water-soluble dyes that have glycol ether added; alcohol-soluble dyes; and oil-soluble dyes mixed with lacquer thinner. Since most water-based and water-reducible pigmented stains contain various alcohols, they will usually work as well. Stains containing water or mineral spirits as their solvents will color the wood around paste fillers but will not alter the color of the fillers themselves.

The key to staining water-based paste filler is to apply the stain after the filler is dry but before it is fully cured. Ideally, you should apply the stain within two or three hours after sanding the filler. If you apply the filler late in the day, you can wait until the next morning to apply the stain. However, if you wait much longer than 12 hours after the filler is dry, the stain probably won't take.

One word of caution when using stains over water-based fillers: The solvents in the stain will soften the filler and can lift it out of the pores of the wood. Because of this, the best way to apply the stain is with a spray gun. However, you may be able to brush a thin coat of stain using a very light touch. It is better to use a foam brush, since the bristles on a regular brush will dig into the pores, further increasing the chances that the filler will be stripped from the surface. Whichever way you apply the stain, work with very thin, even coats so you can avoid having to wipe down the surface after the stain is applied. Wiping the freshly stained wood with a rag will almost certainly remove some of the paste filler from the pores.

Using wood putties

In some cases it may be necessary to use wood putties to fill large defects like gaps in joints or nail holes. Obviously putties should be avoided in work that is being finished with a clear topcoat only, since they would be readily noticeable. However, there are some instances when using wood putties is perfectly acceptable. In particular, if the piece will be stained, the patch can often be blended in such a way as to make it

Wood putties include the wax-based cans on the left, the two lacquer-based products in the middle, and the latex, or water-based, compounds on the right.

solvent gives the mixture a workable viscosity. The main difference between putties and paste fillers is the thickness of the mixture, as putties are much thicker and denser. Like all finishing materials, the solvent used as a carrier is determined by the kinds of resins found in the product. Putties can be wax, lacquer, or water based.

Wax putties are really nothing more than soft crayons and are designed to fill holes after the finish has been applied. Lacquer-based putties come premixed and dry fast. However, they have a tendency to shrink and crack, which makes filling large defects difficult and may require the application of several thin layers. Also, despite what the label may say, lacquer-based putties don't take stain very well and they may not be compatible with a water-based topcoat.

Most water-based, or latex, putties dry just about as fast as lacquer-based products, but they offer several advantages. First, they don't shrink nearly as much, which means you can apply them in thicker layers without having to worry about cracking or using multiple coats. Also, water-based putties are much easier to sand and are compatible with just about any type of finish. They also take stains and dyes better than lacquer-based putties and are easier to tint. Finally, they don't have the powerful smell associated with lacquer-based products.

Water-based putties come premixed or in powder form. Premixed putties are quick and easy to use—simply open the can and you're ready to go. However, they will become lumpy or completely hard if the container is not properly sealed after each use. Dry putty has a tendency to form around the lip of the

nearly invisible. Wood putties are also commonly used under painted surfaces to hide nail holes and other imperfections.

No matter how advanced your woodworking skills are, there will be occasions when you need to hide a mistake or defect in the wood. While paste fillers do a good job of filling pores, they don't work very well on large depressions like knots or worm holes. If the crevice is large, you must break out the can of wood putty.

Wood putties are paste-like mixtures that are used to fill large defects before any stain or finish is applied. Like paste fillers, putties consist of pigments, binders, and solvents. The pigments and binders give the putty its bulk while the container, making it imperative that you clean the opening before putting the lid back on. Dry putty cannot be reactivated by adding water, so once a container has hardened it is useless.

Water-based putties that come in powder form work just like their premixed counterparts, except you mix them yourself. Why, you may be wondering, would anyone go to the trouble of making his own water-based putties when he could buy it already mixed? First, by mixing the powder in a paper cup or disposable container, you'll never be faced with a half of a can of hardened putty that has to be thrown out. Also, mixing your own gives you greater flexibility in how thick or thin the mixture is. For example, if I'm filling one or two large voids, I make the mix thick. If I have to fill a hundred tiny nail holes, I make the mix thinner by adding more water.

MIXING WATER-BASED PUTTIES

When mixing water-based putties, start with a clean cup or container. I use plastic cups that can be washed and reused, but a paper cup or coffee can lid works just as well. It doesn't really matter if you add water to the powder or powder to the water. The thing to keep in mind is that a tiny drop of water goes a long way. The first time I mixed my own water-based putty, I put a heaping teaspoon of powder in a glass and then poured in what I thought was a small amount of water. After stirring, I was left with a mix that had the consistency of chicken broth. No problem, I thought, I'll just add more powder. In went a little powder, then a little more, and a little more. By the time the putty reached the right consistency, I had a batch that

When mixing your own wood putty, be careful how much water you use. This tiny spoonful of water is more than enough to mix this amount of powder.

nearly filled the glass. The problem was I only needed enough to fill a few nail holes.

Now when I mix my own putties I am careful to start with the amount of powder I think I'll need and then add water a few drops at a time, always mixing the water in thoroughly. It is much quicker and easier to thin the mix by adding more water than it is to thicken it by adding powder.

TINTING PUTTIES

If your project will be painted or coated with pigmented lacquer, the color of the putty you use doesn't matter. However, when using clear topcoats, the color of the putty is critical. Nothing looks worse than a patch that is wildly different in color from the surrounding background.

If you plan to finish your project with a clear topcoat and no stain, it helps to start with a shade of putty that is as close to the natural color of the wood as possible. Keep in mind that just because a can of putty is labeled "mahogany" it does not automatically make it the right choice when patching a piece of mahogany. You may be better off using a lighter color, like "oak" or "cherry" and then tinting it to match the piece of wood you are patching. To do this, first wet the wood with water or mineral spirits. This will approximate how the final clear finish will appear. Then, tint the putty using the same methods and materials as outlined on pp. 45-46, keeping in mind that it is easier to darken the color than to lighten it.

If you plan to stain the piece you are patching, you may have a little more work to do. Although most water-based putties take stain relatively well, they are still not perfect. Since you must match the putty to the stained wood, you must first determine if the putty will take more stain than the surrounding wood, thereby appearing darker, or if it will take less stain, looking lighter. Once you have determined how the putty takes the stain (on scrap pieces, of course), you can adjust the color to achieve a better match.

If you do have to tint putty, keep in mind that tinting compounds are pigments that tend to make the putty thicker and harder to work. The more pigment you add to the putty, the thicker it will get. If you find the putty has become too thick to use, simply add a little water to thin it out.

APPLYING PUTTIES

Although I have found that the best tool for applying putty is, appropriately enough, a putty knife, I also use plastic spatulas, thin rippings of wood, and even my fingers. Whichever tool you choose, try to apply the putty sparingly. Ideally you want to force enough putty into the defect to slightly overfill it. This will compensate for any shrinkage while allowing you to sand the dry patch flush with the surface of the wood. If a hole is especially wide or deep, two or three thin coats won't shrink or crack as much as one thick one.

On clear or stained furniture, apply the putty before the last step in your sanding schedule. Let the putty dry thoroughly, then sand the patch along with the rest of the piece. You should be able to tell if the putty is dry by its appearance and how it sands. As water-based putty dries, it lightens in color. Any wet spots will appear dark. Also, wet spots will ball up or crumble when sanded. Dry putty, on the other hand, should feel hard and sand just as the surrounding wood.

On furniture that will be covered with an opaque topcoat, like paint or pigmented lacquer, I generally don't apply wood putty until after the first coat of primer. Primer acts as a bonding agent and helps the putty stick to the wood. Although the putty will normally stick fine on its own, I want any repairs to last, so I feel every little bit helps. Perhaps even more important, the first

One way to cover defects is to fill them with a drop of glue, then sand dust from the surrounding wood into the glue before it is fully dry. Notice how the crack in the glue joint (left) on this turned cylinder virtually disappears (right).

coat of primer causes even the tiniest defects to jump out at you. By waiting until after the primer has been applied, you will ideally only have to go through one round of filling and patching with putty. (For more on patching painted finishes, see Chapter 9.)

MAKING YOUR OWN PUTTIES

An alternative to store-bought putties is to make your own from glue and sawdust. Simply take a few drops of glue and mix in a bunch of fine dust. While this is an easy and inexpensive way to make a decent patch, I have found that no matter how much sawdust you add and how thick you make the mixture, the glue simply will not allow the patch to take the stain or finish very well. The repaired area almost always looks lighter.

Fortunately, there is a quick and easy alternative that usually makes small cracks and nail holes virtually disappear.

First, squeeze a tiny amount of glue into the void. Be sure to use enough glue to fill the hole but don't use so much that it makes a mess of the surrounding wood. Let the glue set for a few minutes, then take a piece of 220-grit sandpaper and begin lightly sanding the area on and around the defect. The fine sawdust that is generated will begin to stick to the glue, eventually covering it completely. Because you are using dust from the wood immediately surrounding the defect, the color is the same and the void seems to disappear. Plus, because the dust is stuck to the glue and not mixed with it, it takes stain and finish pretty much the same as the surrounding wood. Just be sure to thoroughly sand any excess glue off the surface of the wood, otherwise it will show through the finish. While I don't recommend this for large defects, it does work well on small nail holes, cracks, and voids.

5

Sealers

A sales rep from a major finishing manufacturer stopped by my shop one day in the hopes of selling me his line of products. When I told him I preferred water-based finishes, he became quite excited and proceeded to tell me all about their newest water-based topcoats. When I asked him if they made a sealer for these products, he said, "Sure, we make a sanding sealer, but you don't need it."

"If you don't need it," I asked, "why do you make it?"

This was probably the first time anyone had asked him this question, and it was obvious he didn't know quite what to say. He stared at me blankly for a second and then, with an air of authority, stated, "Some people like to use sanding sealers because they are easier to sand."

I smiled and didn't push for any further explanation, but later I thought how this exchange typified the confusion and lack of knowledge surrounding sealers. There is no question that sealers play an important role in finishing. However, for many woodworkers the reasons for using sealers may be somewhat of a mystery. Knowing what sealers are, how they work, and when and how to use them are all important when selecting the right sealer.

Technically, the sales rep was right when he said I didn't really need to use a sealer with his product. No matter what the finish is, the first coat applied to the surface of the wood is a sealer. Although there are some water-based finishes that do a good job of acting like a sealer, (often referred to as "self-sealing"), most of them don't. Most finishes do not contain enough bulk to do a good job of filling pores. As a result, the final finish may appear rough or bumpy. Plus, most clear finishes, paints, and pigmented lacquers will not seal in surface impurities like wax, grease, and knots. No matter how many coats of paint you put over a knot or a crayon mark, it will eventually bleed through. Finally, often a finish used without a sealer won't bond to the bare wood very well. The resulting coating will be easily chipped or marred and in some cases may peel off the wood. In addition, if you have used a water-soluble dye on your project, a coat of clear finish may redissolve the dye, causing it to lift off the surface or bleed into the topcoat.

What are sealers?

Sealers really are nothing more than a clear finish that has been altered to make it perform differently. What is added, or removed, from the finish determines what the sealer is and what it does. For example, sanding sealer is a clear finish that has stearates added to it. Stearates are simply soapy minerals that make the finish easier to sand. (They are, in fact, the same minerals found on stearated sandpaper.) Primer, which is the sealer used with paints and pigmented lacquers, is basically paint or lacquer that has an increased amount of pigment. The additional pigment helps the primer bond to wood better than the paint or lacquer would by itself.

In simple terms, sealers do just what their name implies: They seal the surface of the wood, preventing it from absorbing any stain, dye, paint, or clear

Some water-based products, like the production lacquer on the right and the dual-purpose finish on the left, are self-sealing.

finish. However, when used properly sealers are capable of doing a lot more than simply stopping up the pores of the wood or making the raised grain easier to sand. They can be used as barrier coats to seal in surface impurities like dirt, wax, silicone, and natural oils, preventing them from leaking out of the wood and through the finish. Sealers can also be applied in thin washcoat layers between two different finish materials, eliminating the chance of one material dissolving or bleeding into another. And finally, sealers can act as bonding agents between two materials that may not normally adhere to one another. This is especially important when working with water-based finishes that may not be compatible with solvent-based products.

Sounds easy, doesn't it? Well, naturally there's more to it than that. Since most manufacturers design their sealers to work with their own topcoats, different sealers are designed to do different things. Plus, how well a sealer performs depends not only on the sealer itself but also on how it is applied. Knowing what sealers are, how they work, and when to use them are all important to understanding the role they may play in a finishing schedule.

SEALERS AS PORE FILLERS

The most obvious reason to use a sealer is to seal the pores of the wood. This not only prevents the wood from absorbing any more finish but also helps to create an even surface that is easy to sand flat and smooth. Sealers contain additives such as stearates that are not found in clear finishes. Stearates add volume to the sealer, which allows the film to build quickly without making the sealer itself thick or hard to apply. In fact, most sealers are thinner and easier to work with than clear topcoats.

The drawback to these additives is that they are relatively cloudy and don't dry very hard. In most cases, one coat of properly applied sealer should be all you need to fully seal the surface of the wood. Occasionally, you may need to use a second coat, but I would never use more than that.

SEALERS AS BARRIER COATS

In addition to preventing finish from getting *in* the wood, sealers may also be used to prevent impurities from sneaking *out*. Some of these impurities may occur naturally, like resin, oils, and knots. Others, such as grease, wax, silicone, and old finish, may be man-made. However impurities get there, they all have one thing in common: If left unsealed they will inevitably bleed through and mar or even ruin a finish. Using vinyl sealers and shellac will stop up the wood's pores, forming a continuous film that is virtually impenetrable from either direction. Not only will the wood be incapable of absorbing more finish, but whatever is under the sealer will remain trapped there, unable to work its way through to the topcoat.

SEALERS AS WASHCOATS

Another way in which sealers are used is to act as "screens" between various coatings. This proves especially valuable when working with water-soluble dyes, which have a tendency to redissolve when another coat of water-based material is placed over them. Introducing a coat of sealer between coats of dye or between coats of dye and clear finish will prevent one coat from bleeding into the next. This washcoat not only acts as a buffer between materials but also reduces the chances of cutting through an underlying layer of finish when sanding the next coat.

SEALERS AS BONDING AGENTS

Each step of a finishing schedule directly affects the step that comes next. Skipping a step in the interest of saving time or substituting an inferior product to save a few dollars may have disastrous effects on the outcome of the final finish. Above all, the fillers, stains, sealers, and topcoats you use must all be compatible with one another, otherwise the finish may at some point fail. If you are using strictly solvent-based products through every step of the finishing process, you need not be concerned whether one product is compatible with the next.

However, with water-based products compatibility becomes more of an issue. Although these products have improved greatly over the years, you may still encounter circumstances where a water-based product simply will not adhere to a solvent-based material. Ideally, if you know you will be working with a water-based topcoat you should try to use water-based products throughout the finishing process. Using water-based paste fillers, water-soluble dyes, and water-based sealers and topcoats will greatly simplify matters. And yet, there are bound to be occasions when you will be mixing solvent-based and water-based products on the same piece. As long as you take certain precautions, you should find that adhesion problems are a thing of the past.

The best way to determine whether two finish materials are compatible is simple: Make a test piece. Be sure that you follow the same procedure when finishing your test piece as you will when finishing your project. Use the same wood, the same finish materials, and the same application equipment. Let the various coats of finish dry the same amount of time, and use the same sanding procedures. Once the sample piece is complete, check for proper adhesion by scoring the finish with a knife and seeing if any peels or flakes off. You could also check adhesion by pressing a piece of tape over the finish. When the tape is pulled off, the finish should stay on the wood. If the finish pulls off the wood and sticks to the tape, you've got an adhesion problem. If so, it may be a good idea to reevaluate your finishing materials and methods.

Sometimes adhesion problems become apparent immediately. In extreme cases, the finish will bead up and won't flow out properly. Other times problems won't show until a few hours after the finish is dry. The topcoat may blister or crack and will appear to be pulling away from whatever is underneath it. Sometimes the problem won't appear for several days or even weeks after the finish is applied. In this worst case scenario, which is every professional finisher's nightmare, the finish may begin to crack or even pull away from the coating or wood in large strips or sheets. While this was not uncommon a few years ago, water-based products have fortunately improved to the point where this should no longer be a problem.

When applying water-based topcoats over solvent-based fillers and stains, give the solvent-based product plenty of time to cure. Keep in mind the difference between cured and dry. A pigmented stain may be dry to the touch in a matter of a few minutes or hours, but it will not be fully cured until all of the solvent has evaporated. I once made the mistake of spraying a coat of water-based finish over a piece that had been given a coat of solvent-based stain after letting the stain dry for only a few hours. The next day the topcoat started to bubble and peel off in sheets.

If your test piece shows there may be a compatibility problem, you have two choices: Switch your finishing materials completely or apply a bonding agent between the two incompatible products. Most manufacturers make sealers that are specifically intended to be bonding agents. The sealers are designed to be used with the manufacturers' products and will, in most cases, eliminate adhesion problems.

Appropriate sealers for water-based products include water-based sanding sealers (left), vinyl sealers (middle), and shellac (right).

Types of sealers

The most common types of sealers you will encounter when working with water-based products are sanding sealers, vinyl sealers, shellac, and pigmented primers. Although in general these sealers perform the same basic functions, they do contain different properties that may make one a better choice than the others in certain situations.

SANDING SEALERS

Most water-based finishes are relatively scratch resistant, which means they are also relatively difficult to sand. Sanding sealers are designed to make it easy to obtain a smooth surface without a lot of work. Sanding sealers are basically clear topcoats that have metal stearates added to them. These soapy compounds soften the sealer, making it easier to sand. Stearates also help the sealer build fast

but make a poor finish when used too heavily. In such a case, the resulting film will be relatively soft and may appear somewhat cloudy.

Many water-based sanding sealers are also designed to raise the grain of the wood. When the sealer is dry, the raised fibers are stiffened and easier to sand, or knock down. The resulting surface is smooth and will take subsequent coats of finish without any more grain being raised. Some manufacturers also use their sanding sealers as a means of imparting color to the underlying wood, giving it the amber look associated with traditional solvent-based materials. They do this by adding small amounts of tint or pigment to the sealer.

VINYL SEALERS

A second type of sealer you may encounter when working with water-based topcoats derives its name from the vinyl modified resins used to make it. These resins make vinyl sealers much tougher than sanding sealers, creating an impenetrable film that will not allow anything to pass through. This may be helpful if you are trying to layer multiple coats of water-soluble dyes to create special colors or effects and are worried about one coat bleeding into another. Vinyl sealers may also be a good choice when combining finishes that would not ordinarily be compatible. One cabinet-maker I've worked with uses vinyl sealers under water-based topcoats because, as he puts it, the sealer "punches up" the color of the wood, making the resulting finish look more like nitrocellulose lacquer. Another furniture maker I know uses a lot of veneers in his work. He uses vinyl sealer under water-based topcoats because he is afraid the water in the finish might cause the veneer to bubble or swell.

In theory, vinyl sealers may sound like the ideal product. However, they are not without their problems. Some sealers must be recoated within a certain time period. If you wait too long to apply the topcoat, it may not adhere properly and the finish will delaminate or peel off. For this reason, it is a good idea to read the application instructions thoroughly and follow the manufacturer's recommendations to the letter. If you have any questions, call the manufacturer and ask them. Most companies have technical support numbers on the can and are more than willing to provide information. Above all, if you are unsure of how a vinyl sealer will work, do a few test pieces first.

Although vinyl sealers do have some attractive properties, I generally try to avoid them in my shop. I have found

The left half of this board was coated with untinted sanding sealer, while the right side was finished with sealer that was mixed with a few drops of burnt sienna tint. Notice how the tint helps give the wood the amber look associated with solvent-based finishes.

they can be tricky to apply and often don't work as promised.

SHELLAC
You are probably wondering why an alcohol-based product is being mentioned in a book on water-based finishes. The answer is simple: For my money shellac is the finest sealer made. It is easily brushed or sprayed, dries fast, and sands well. Fresh, dewaxed shellac is also an excellent bonding agent. In fact, it is probably the best bonding agent available. It can be used over, under, and between just about any type of filler, stain, dye, and topcoat. As an added bonus, shellac helps give wood the warm, amber color associated with solvent-based finishes that is often lacking in water-based products.

Used as a sealer, shellac prevents water-soluble dyes from redissolving and bleeding into the next coat of dye or clear finish. Used as a bonding agent, it

Vinyl sealers: A cautionary tale

A few years ago, I was called in to help build some cabinets for a large, new home. The primary cabinetmaker was having trouble meeting the delivery schedule, so I was asked to build a few vanities and various built-in units. I was told to match the design and look of the other cabinetmaker's work as closely as possible.

When the cabinets were installed, the owner complained that the color of the finish was not right. After taking a closer look, I realized that although I did a pretty good job of matching my water-based pigmented lacquer to the precatalyzed lacquer the other cabinetmaker was using, the color was a bit off. The owner and architect both made it clear that they would only be happy if I used the exact same finish that was used throughout the rest of the house. I agreed to come back to the house and refinish the units in place. Fortunately, the other cabinetmaker agreed to sell me some of the lacquer he was using, thereby guaranteeing the color would match.

I was somewhat concerned that the solvent-based lacquer would not adhere to the water-based finish, so I called the manufacturers of both products for advice. They agreed that under no circumstances should I apply the precatalyzed lacquer directly over the dried water-based finish. The only way they could see this working was if I applied a barrier coat of vinyl sealer first.

Before I spent a whole day refinishing the cabinets, I decided to do a simple test. I finished a scrap piece with the water-based product I had originally used and let it dry for several days. I then applied the vinyl sealer to half of the board and, after letting it dry according to the instructions on the can, sprayed a coat of the precatalyzed lacquer over the entire piece. The next day the results were the exact opposite of what I was led to expect. The finish that was applied directly over the water-based finish adhered with no problems, while the side with the vinyl sealer showed almost no adhesion at all. In fact, I was able to remove the finish simply by rubbing it with my finger. I made another test piece just to be sure I hadn't done something wrong, but the results were the same.

I let the unsealed half of the test boards sit for more than a week before checking them again for any signs of cracking or peeling, and, much to my relief, I saw no signs of adhesion problems.

From this experience I learned two things. First, finishes are funny products that do not always do what you expect or work as advertised. Second, when in doubt about mixing various types of finishes, always do a few test pieces.

---

allows finish materials that may otherwise be incompatible to be used together without adhesion problems. As a sanding sealer, it raises the grain while stiffening the fibers, making sanding easy. In short, shellac is indispensable when working with water-based finishes.

However, shellac is not foolproof, and if you don't take certain precautions it may end up causing more problems than it solves. Shellac, which is made from the secretions of a tiny bug found in India and Thailand, contains naturally occurring wax. The wax adds color and volume, but it also makes the finish

Shellac as a sealer

Pros

- Easy to apply.

- Compatible with all finishes.

- Dries quickly.

- Sands easily.

- Seals in defects like knots, grease, stripper residue, wax, and silicone.

Cons

- Alcohol is flammable.

- Have to mix your own or wait for wax to settle.

- Limited shelf life.

softer and less water resistant. More important, wax will inhibit the shellac's ability to act as a bonding agent, especially when dealing with finishes containing urethane resins.

Fortunately, you can buy shellac that has had practically all of the wax removed. Dewaxed shellac, usually called super blonde, is sold in flakes that must be mixed with alcohol. The resulting finish is relatively pure, consisting of at most 1% wax.

Mixing shellac Mixing your own shellac is easy and guarantees you will always have a fresh supply. Simply mix an appropriate quantity of flakes with alcohol. Technically, any alcohol will dissolve shellac, but denatured alcohol is the best choice. Denatured alcohol is ethanol, or grain alcohol, that has poisons added to make it undrinkable and therefore not subject to liquor taxes. This means it is not only relatively inexpensive but readily available in paint

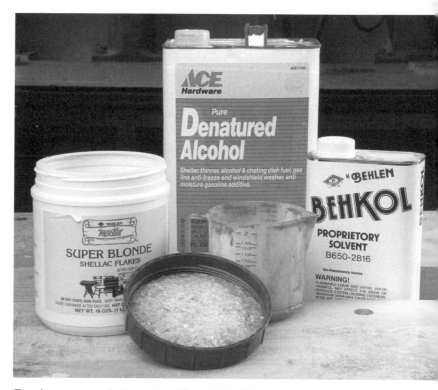

To mix your own shellac, you will need the flakes, a measuring cup, a clean container, and alcohol.

The cut refers to the ratio of shellac to alcohol. Compare the color of the 3-pound cut on the left with the 1-pound cut on the right.

and hardware stores. You can also buy special shellac thinners that are mainly ethanol with small amounts of slower drying alcohols added. By slowing down the drying time of shellac, these products give you a bit more time to work, which comes in handy when applying shellac with a brush.

The ratio of dried flakes to alcohol will determine how thick or what "cut" the shellac is. For example, a 3-pound cut contains 3 pounds of shellac in 1 gallon of alcohol. When using shellac as a sealer, I generally find a 2-pound cut (2 pounds of flakes in 1 gallon of alcohol) works well. The shellac is thick enough to seal the wood but thin enough to flow on well and dry fast. In some cases, when using the shellac simply as a sanding sealer, I work with a 1-pound cut. This relatively thin mixture applies easily, dries incredibly fast, and raises the

grain and stiffens the fibers, making them easy to sand smooth.

All shellacs have a limited lifespan. As they grow old they lose their ability to dry. This is especially true of dewaxed shellac. As a result, it is a good idea to mix only what you need. If you do mix your own shellac, use a glass container, as metal cans will react with the alcohol and may change the color of the solution.

The beauty of shellac is that you don't have to be a chemist to mix up a batch. If your 2-pound cut ends up as a 1¾-pound or 2⅛-pound mix, it doesn't really matter. Using a scale to weigh the flakes will ensure accuracy, but I usually mix batches by volume and often by eye. For a 2-pound cut, put ¼ pound of flakes in a 1-quart glass jar, then add 1 pint of alcohol. The flakes will take at least 24 hours to fully dissolve and maybe as much as two or three days, so it pays to plan ahead. Stir the solution frequently during the course of the day, and keep moisture out of the jar by putting the lid on tight when not stirring. If you need the shellac in a hurry, you can speed up the process by breaking up the flakes into a fine powder and submerging the container in warm water. Remember that alcohol is extremely flammable, so never use a stove, oven, or open flame to warm the mixture.

It is a good idea to label the container with the date the shellac was mixed to help you avoid using shellac that has been sitting around for too long. In general, I never use shellac that is more than six months old. If you are not sure how old the shellac is, put a few drops on a piece of metal or glass and see how it dries. If it dries hard within

10 minutes, it is okay to use. If it is gummy or sticky after 10 minutes, it is suspect. If, after several hours, it still hasn't dried, it is definitely no good. I once tried to get by with a jar that had been sitting on the shelf for more than a year, and I ended up having to peel off the subsequent finish, sand down to bear wood, and start over again. From that day on, my policy toward suspect shellac has been, "When in doubt, throw it out."

Using premixed shellac If you don't use a lot of shellac, you may not want to go through the trouble of buying the flakes and mixing your own. If this is the case, you can buy premixed shellac and dewax it yourself. Most ready-made shellacs are sold in a 3-pound cut and come in clear or amber. While you could use amber, I prefer clear. I have found that the wax in amber shellac is not only hard to see but also takes a long time to settle out of the solution. Plus, the shellac is being used as a sealer, not to radically change the color of the wood.

Dewaxing the shellac is simply a matter of letting the can sit for a while until the wax, which will appear cloudy or even murky, settles to the bottom. The resulting clear liquid floating on top is relatively pure shellac. How long this takes will depend on how much the can was agitated beforehand. It may take a day for most of the wax to settle out or it may take a week. On occasions when I have run out of shellac in the middle of the job, I have been able to buy a can off the shelf, reaching way in the back for a can that probably wasn't handled recently, gingerly carry it back to my shop, and pour at least a small amount of relatively clear liquid off the top.

Keep in mind that the dewaxed shellac is still the same cut as it was

If you let a jar of clear shellac sit undisturbed for a day or two, the wax will settle to the bottom, leaving relatively pure shellac floating on top.

before you got rid of the wax. If the premixed can was a 3-pound cut, the resulting pure liquid will also be a 3-pound cut. To cut it further, simply add the proper amount of alcohol.

Be careful when you siphon off the clear shellac, since it doesn't take much to get the wax stirred back into the mix. You could run the shellac through a tightly woven mesh cloth, but you would have to repeat the process numerous times to get rid of all the wax. Be sure to label the jar with the date so you can keep track of how old the newly dewaxed shellac is. Although the manufacturer may claim the shellac will last for up to three years, I would be careful when using anything older than six months.

Finally, if you do use this method to make your own dewaxed shellac, don't

Pigmented primers, whether designed for use with paint or lacquer, are nothing more than opaque sealers.

be surprised if you are left with half a can of wax. In fact, on at least one occasion I started with 1 gallon of clear shellac and ended up with 1 quart of usable material and 3 quarts of wax. While this may not sound like an economical approach to buying dewaxed shellac, it is an alternative to mixing your own.

PIGMENTED PRIMERS

Up to this point, I've focused on clear sealers used with stained or natural finishes. However, pigmented primers are also available. Pigmented primers are nothing more than clear sealers that have pigments and flatting agents like talc added to make them opaque. They are used under paint or pigmented lacquers and perform the same functions as any clear sealer. The only difference is that you would not use a primer between

layers of the topcoat the way you might use a clear sealer between multiple coats of dyes and topcoats. (For more on primers, see Chapter 8.)

Applying sealers

With a few exceptions, sealers are applied just as an ordinary topcoat. The main difference is in how thick the coat is applied and how it is sanded. Most sealers are designed to be applied in thin coats. Because they are relatively soft, they are not meant to be built up as part of the finish. If you were to place a sheet of glass over a piece of foam rubber and then step on it, the rubber would give and the glass would break. Similarly, if you use sealer to build up a thick layer of soft, flexible finish and then place a relatively hard topcoat over it, the topcoat may eventually crack or craze. Shellac is the one sealer that can be built up under the finish without any adverse effects. Although thick coats of shellac will take longer to dry and may require more sanding than thin coats, putting on too much won't harm the finish.

BRUSHING SEALERS

Whether you use a brush or foam applicator will depend entirely on the type and brand sealer you use. Some water-based products can be brushed, while others are designed to be sprayed. Likewise, most vinyl sealers are intended to be applied with spray equipment. Shellac, on the other hand, can be applied with a brush quite easily. If you do brush shellac, you will have to work quickly. Because it dries so fast, you won't have much opportunity to go back and even out brushstrokes. As a result, you should select a good-quality natural-bristle brush that is firm and holds a lot of liquid. On the upper end of the price scale are fitch brushes, which are made of skunk hair. The next choice would be a china bristle brush.

While synthetic-bristle brushes will work, they won't do as good a job as natural-bristle brushes of applying a smooth, even coat. Obviously, the smoother the coat goes on, the less work you will have to do to get a good finish. However, if you're applying a thin 1- or 2-pound cut of shellac, you can use just about any kind of brush without too many worries. The resulting coat will be so easy to sand that you should be able to make brush or lap marks disappear with very little effort.

With water-based sealers, the choice of brushes is a bit more important. While you could use a natural-bristle brush, the bristles will absorb the water and begin to splay or fray. The brush will gradually become very hard to use, won't hold its shape, and will begin to leave marks all over the work. When brushing any type of water-based finishes, select a good-quality synthetic-bristle brush. (For more on brushes, see Chapter 7.) Synthetic bristles won't absorb the water and lose their shape, making them not only easier to use but also easier to clean.

Because sealers dry fast, you won't have much time to correct any problems resulting from the wrong choice of brush. However, like shellac, water-based sealers are easy to sand, so if your seal coat is not perfect don't be overly concerned.

The techniques for brushing sealers are the same regardless of what the sealer is and what type of brush you use. Begin by wetting the brush with the appropriate solvent. Dip the brush all the way up to the ferrule in alcohol (if you are using shellac) or in water (if you are using a water-based sealer). This will not only prime the brush and make it easier to use but will also make cleaning up much easier.

Because sealers dry fast, work quickly. Dip the brush about one-third to one-half the way into the finish, then apply the sealer using long, even strokes. Although it may be difficult to maintain a wet edge when brushing sealers, try to nonetheless. Overlap each pass a bit, always working from where your last pass ended. You may be tempted to go back and "tip off" the finish as you would with slower-drying topcoats, but don't bother. With most water-based sealers and shellac, spending too much time trying to even out the finish won't do much good. It is best to flow the material on and leave it alone. Some of the brush marks may disappear as the finish dries, and those that don't will be easily removed by sanding.

SPRAYING SEALERS

With a few minor exceptions, I can't really think of anything I do differently when spraying sealers than when spraying topcoats. I rarely make any adjustments to the fluid tip, air cap, or settings on the gun, and the mechanics of how the material is applied are pretty much the same. I do work much quicker when spraying sealers and primers and tend to apply the seal coat a bit thinner than I would a topcoat. There should never be any need to add thinner to a clear sealer, but you may have to add thinner or flow additive to pigmented primers. In fact, the primer I use in my shop is so thick that I not only add thinner, but I also have to increase the fluid pressure on the pot to get the material to spray properly.

Sanding sealers

Generally sealers don't require a lot of heavy sanding. In fact, oversanding a seal coat is not a good idea, since you may end up removing the sealer entirely and cutting through the stain, dye, or paste filler below. If the sealer is used over bare wood, you don't have to be quite as careful, but you should still avoid sanding it all off. The objective when sanding seal coats is to create a smooth, even surface by removing raised grain and any surface defects like brush marks, bubbles, and dust. The grit paper you use and how hard you have to work really depends on how good a job you did preparing the wood and applying the sealer. In my shop, we usually sand seal coats with 240-grit wet/dry paper. In production situations, we use a palm sander to knock down the grain and smooth the surface. Usually two or three quick passes with the sander over an area is all that is needed to prepare the surface for the next coat. Using this method, we are able to sand several thousand linear feet of material in a matter of a few hours.

When working on finer pieces, take a bit more care in how you sand the seal coat. I still use 240-grit paper, but I am sure to work slowly and thoroughly over the entire piece. Although I may still use an electric sander on large areas, I generally prefer to sand the sealer by hand, using a block of wood to back the paper.

Though stearated papers will make sanding a bit easier, most sealers are so easy to sand that you probably won't need them. Because these papers may leave particles of stearates on the surface of the wood that can cause fisheye, you must be careful to wipe all sanding residue away before continuing with the next coat of finish.

When sealers are fully dry, they are a joy to sand. The raised grain should disappear effortlessly, and the sealer should form a soft, dry powdery substance. The paper will feel almost as if it is gliding over the surface, with very little drag or friction. If the sealer does not turn to powder or if the paper begins to streak or gum up, the sealer is not dry. If this happens, you may have to spot-coat the area that was sanded and wait for the entire surface to dry before trying again.

The paper on the left is loaded with gummy sealer that was sanded before it had a chance to dry. The paper on the right is coated with a fine powder typical of dry sealer.

6

Stains and Dyes

Once your project has been sanded and the pores are filled, you are faced with your next finishing decision: Should the wood be stained or finished with a clear topcoat only? Stains and dyes offer little or no protection for the wood, so the answer depends entirely on personal preference. Some pieces of furniture and types of wood may look better stained, while others are best left natural.

Once you have decided on coloring a project, the next step is deciding whether to use a pigmented stain or a dye. In general, both perform the same function: They change the color of the wood. However, the way they are made and how they appear on the surface of the wood are very different.

Oil-based pigmented stains

As their name implies, pigmented stains contain pigments that color the wood. The pigments are relatively large particles that become lodged in the nooks and crannies on the surface of the wood. These include the open pores and scratches left by sanding. In addition to the pigment, these stains contain a solvent, or carrier, and binders. The solvent is what gives the stain its viscosity, making it workable, while the binder holds the pigment together on the surface of the wood after it dries. Without a binder, the dried pigments, which may be natural minerals or synthetic powders, would simply turn back to their original state and blow away.

The left side of this piece of ash was stained with a solvent-based pigmented stain, while the right side was coated with a water-soluble dye. On the side that was stained, there is a marked contrast between the color of the pores and the surrounding wood. Although the grain is still clearly visible on the side that was dyed, the wood is more evenly colored and the contrast between the pores and the surrounding wood is not as great.

PIGMENTED STAINS

Pigmented stains contain large particles of colorant that lodge in the crevices and pores of the wood.

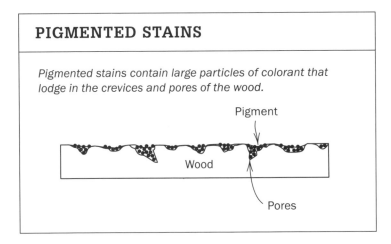

Commercially available products may use alkyd resins or tung or linseed oil as binders and mineral spirits as the solvent. The pigments are suspended, or floating, in this solution. When the stain is applied, the solvent evaporates, leaving behind the binders and particles of pigment. The pigments become lodged in the open pores of the wood and are locked in place by the binders.

ADVANTAGES OF OIL-BASED PIGMENTED STAINS

Pigmented stains have many advantages over dye stains. They come premixed and are easy to use. You don't have to worry about mixing the right amounts, and you don't need any special measuring equipment. This not only makes life simpler but also ensures a consistency in color from one can of stain to the next. Just stir them and they are ready to use.

The pigments used in these stains are opaque, which means they reflect light. As a result, they are very resistant to fading when exposed to sunlight. The opacity of the pigments also means they tend to hide or obscure the underlying wood. While pigmented stains may not be a good choice on a highly figured piece of maple or mahogany, they can be used quite effectively to mask the less attractive grain found on an inferior species of wood. In fact, many large furniture manufacturers achieve their "cherry wood finish" by applying layers of pigmented stains over beech or birch.

Finally, because the pigments are lodged in the open pores of the wood, they can be used quite effectively to highlight the grain of ring porous woods such as ash and red oak.

DISADVANTAGES OF OIL-BASED PIGMENTED STAINS

Like all finishes, pigmented stains are far from perfect. Because the particles of pigment are relatively large, they tend to lodge in pores and scratches more than in the surrounding wood. This leads to two potential problems. First, the surface of open-grained woods, like red oak, and the end grain of any species of wood may be colored unevenly. Second, defects such as large sanding scratches, dings, and other blemishes are not hidden by the stain but tend to be highlighted.

Although the opacity of pigmented stains can be an advantage in some cases, it is viewed as a problem in others. The opacity tends to make the pigments appear muddy, obscuring the underlying wood. Pigmented stains are, in effect, highly thinned paints, and they often give a nice piece of wood a dull, lifeless look.

Another problem with oil-based stains is that they may not always be compatible with water-based topcoats. Although water-based finishes have improved to where adhesion over oil-

The bottom door frame was stained with a solvent-based pigmented product. Notice how the end grain appears much darker than the side grain. The contrast between the end and side grain on the top frame, which was coated with a water-soluble dye, is much less noticeable.

Pigmented stains (top) draw attention to surface defects like these exaggerated sanding scratches. Dyes (bottom) color the scratches and the surrounding wood more evenly. Although the scratches are still visible, they do not appear as dramatic when contrasted with the surrounding wood.

based products is usually not much of a problem, there are still certain precautions worth taking. The oil-based product must not only be dry to the touch but also completely cured, which may take anywhere from overnight to two to three days. In some cases, you may need to apply a barrier coat of sealer between the two products to ensure proper adhesion. The only way to know for sure if a water-based topcoat will stick to an oil-based pigmented stain is to try a test piece first.

Another drawback to oil-based pigmented stains is they are smelly to use and messy to clean up. To clean your brushes and spray equipment, you will need to use mineral spirits, which must be stored and disposed of properly. Plus, if you do a lot of staining, you will go through a fair amount of rags.

Water-based stains

If you like using pigmented stains but don't like the smell or mess of using solvent-based products, there is an alternative. Over the past few years several finish manufacturers have introduced water-based pigmented stains, which use water as the solvent, or carrier. Like oil-based stains, they contain pigments, or acrylic colorants, and binders that are mixed in the carrier. Many of these water-based stains also contain dyes, which help color the wood more evenly.

Water-based stains offer many advantages over oil-based products. Because they are absorbed deeper and more evenly, they appear clearer and brighter in color and don't obscure the figure of the wood the way oil-based

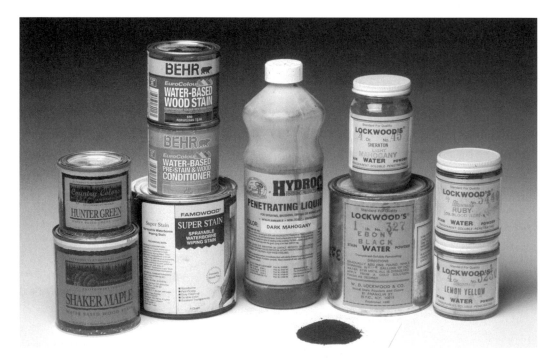

Water-based stains include wiping stains, nongrain-raising dyes, and water-soluble dye powders.

products often do. They can be easily thinned or reduced with water and can be applied with a rag, brush, or spray gun. Plus, they aren't as smelly or nearly as toxic or flammable as oil-based stains.

a lot messier than with brushes. For this reason, when using rags it is a good idea to wear protective gloves, otherwise you will end up with as much color on your hands as you do on the wood.

Applying stains

The beauty of stains and dyes is that they are all applied in pretty much the same way: Flood the surface and wipe off the excess. How you do this is a matter of personal preference. You can use rags, spray guns, brushes, sponges, foam brushes, pads, and rollers to apply them.

RAGS

The most common ways to apply stains are with rags, brushes, and foam brushes. I prefer using rags for a few reasons. First, they hold a lot of stain, making it easy to flood a heavy coat on the surface. In addition to making the staining go quickly, rags also make it easier to move the stain around and work it into the surface of the wood. Plus, when you are done with a rag, you can simply let it dry on a flat surface, then throw it out. (Never throw wet rags in a garbage pail—they may spontaneously combust.) Although you will go through a lot of rags, using them cuts down on the time and mess involved with cleaning brushes.

Rags do have their problems though. They often leave behind little pieces of thread and lint that can become trapped in the finish coat. It is also difficult to reach inside corners with rags. Finally, although the final cleanup is easier with rags, the application process is generally

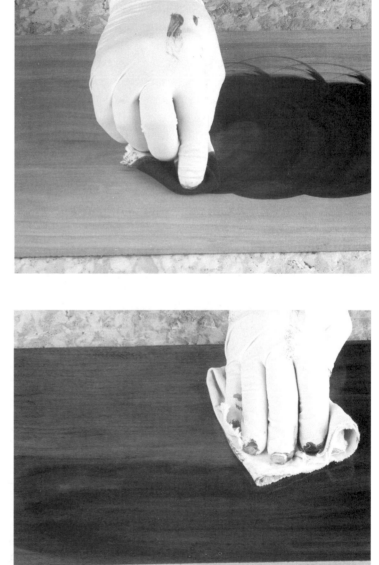

When using rags to apply stain, flood the surface (top), then wipe off the excess (bottom) before it has time to dry.

SPRAY GUNS

If you have a lot of staining to do, you may consider using your spray gun. Although I have on at least one occasion used spray equipment to apply oil-based pigmented stain on large projects, I generally avoid putting these products in my guns. Even with proper ventilation, airborne particles of stain tend to settle on everything, leaving behind a sticky mess. Also, cleaning the equipment after using pigmented stains takes a fair amount of work and can be a chore. However, if you do use a gun, the application process is the same—flood the surface and wipe off the excess.

Many of the newer water-based stains are designed specifically for use with spray guns. They contain additives that make them dry too fast to be applied with rags or brushes. The easiest way to tell if a water-based stain is meant for spraying is to read the label. If the product is called a "wiping stain," it can be sprayed but is really designed to be applied with a brush or rag. In most cases, stains that are meant to be sprayed will say so right on the can.

BRUSHES

Although I don't particularly like using brushes for applying stains, they do have a few advantages over rags. They give you good control over how much stain goes on, as well as where the stain goes. Brushes are also good for reaching into deep corners and intricate carvings or turnings. However, they are slower to use than rags and can be difficult to clean. If you use the same brush to apply stains and topcoats and it is not completely clean, the stain may contaminate the jar of clear finish.

In addition to rags and brushes, stains may be applied with pads, foam brushes, short-nap rollers, and sponges.

SPONGES, FOAM BRUSHES, PADS, AND ROLLERS

If you prefer not to use brushes or rags to apply pigmented stains, you could choose alternatives such as sponges, foam brushes, pads, or even rollers. Sponges work just like rags. They hold a lot of liquid, are easy to use, and do a good job of working the stain around and into the surface of the wood. Plus, they are inexpensive and disposable. However, I have found that it doesn't take very much aggressive rubbing before a sponge begins to shred and fall apart, leaving little bits and pieces stuck all over the wood.

Foam brushes combine some of the best qualities of rags and brushes. Like rags, they hold a lot of fluid, making it easy to flood the surface. Like brushes, they have handles that make them cleaner and easier to use, allowing you to reach into tight places. Plus, they are inexpensive and can be thrown away after use. However, foam brushes are basically sponges on a stick. Like sponges, they begin to fall apart relatively quickly. The weight of the fluid makes the sponge rather flimsy, and the sponge may begin to pull away from the handle long before you are finished staining a large job. For this reason, I only use foam brushes when I am working on small projects.

Finally, if you have a large, flat area to stain, such as paneled walls or a wood floor, your best bet may be to use a pad or a roller. If you do use a roller, be sure it has a short, tight nap. Bulky rollers will absorb and waste a lot of stain and may become soggy and difficult to use.

Dyes

Powdered dyes offer an alternative to pigmented stains. Unlike pigmented stains, which contain large particles of pigment, dyes consist of relatively small particles of colorant that are completely dissolved in an appropriate solvent. Most people have probably heard of aniline dyes. The term aniline refers to a petroleum-based product that was originally used in the 19th century in the manufacturing of dyes. Aniline is toxic, has been linked with cancer, and is no longer used in the production of commercially available dyes. Today, dyes are made of synthetic colored powders that are much safer to use and handle. Although the term aniline dye is still commonly used, rest assured the products available today contain no aniline.

Natural dyes have been used to color wood, paper, and cloth for centuries. Until relatively recently, dyes were made from the colorants found in natural products such as fruit, nut shells, and berries. It wasn't until the second half of the 19th century that chemists developed a way to fabricate dyes from man-made products such as aniline.

The ability to create dyes from artificially synthesized chemicals opened up an entire world of color. No longer were dyes limited to naturally occurring earth tones. Today, you can buy dyes in just about any shade imaginable, including bright primary colors.

ADVANTAGES OF DYES

In one respect, dyes are much simpler than pigmented stains, while on the other hand they are much more

If you apply a dye that is too dark, you can lighten the color by wiping the surface with water (right). Likewise, you can darken the color by applying another coat (left).

complex. Whereas pigmented stains contain pigments, solvents, and binders, dyes are simply colorants dissolved in solvent. However, dyes are more complex than this. Unlike pigmented stains, which need a binder to hold the pigment in place, dyes are absorbed into the molecular structure of the wood, coloring the fibers evenly and deeply. Because dyes are absorbed into the wood, they do not need any binders to lock them in place. This lack of binders means that, unlike pigmented stains, dyes can be at least partially removed from the surface after they have been applied. If you don't like the color or need to lighten it, you can wipe the appropriate solvent onto the surface of the wood. The solvent redissolves the dye, which can then be lifted off the wood with a rag or brush.

Another advantage dyes have over pigmented stains is that the tiny size of

the dye molecules makes dyes transparent. They are absorbed into the wood without obscuring any of the wood's figure. This makes dyes ideal for use over beautifully grained pieces like bird's-eye maple or any of the exquisitely patterned veneers commonly found in fine furniture.

Another advantage to using dyes is that because you mix your own solution, you have much greater control over the depth of color. If you want a lighter shade, simply add more solvent. If the stain is too light, add more dye powder. This ability to adjust a dye's color gives you a much greater degree of flexibility than you have when working with pigmented stains.

Because dyes are absorbed more deeply into the wood than pigmented stains, dyes color the wood more evenly and give the color a greater sense of depth. This makes dyes ideal for evening

The ratio of powder to water determines how concentrated the color of a dye will be. As the amount of water is decreased, the dye gets darker. The dye on the left half of this board was mixed in a ratio of 1 ounce powder to 1 quart water. The right half was finished with the same dye that was cut with another quart of water.

out wildly varying color within a board or for matching end and side grain.

Another major advantage dyes have over their pigmented cousins is they are much easier to repair. If you have ever tried to restain an area finished with a pigmented product that has been cut through by sanding, you have no doubt seen that the stain does not take as well. No matter what you do, the repaired area always seems lighter. With dyes, repairs are virtually invisible. If you cut through the dye to bare wood when sanding, simply apply a bit of the same dye. The dye is absorbed into the wood, coloring the fibers evenly and matching them to the surrounding areas.

Compared to oil-based pigmented products, dyes dry fast and can often be topcoated in a few hours. (Although I wouldn't recommend this, I once sprayed a coat of nitrocellulose lacquer

Dyes do a good job of evening out variances in the color of a piece of wood. As shown in the unfinished end on the left, this cherry board consists of a band of heartwood surrounded by white sapwood. The coat of dye applied on the right evens out the early and late wood, blending them together.

over a dye 10 minutes after it was applied with no noticeable problems.) Dyes are also less expensive than premixed pigmented stains. An ounce of powder used to make a quart of dye may cost $4 or $5, whereas a comparable amount of premixed pigmented stain may cost twice as much.

DISADVANTAGES OF DYES

Although mixing your own dyes gives you greater control over color, it does present problems. Rather than simply pulling a can of stain off the store shelf, you must mix it yourself, which calls for measuring devices and proper storage containers. Maintaining the exact color from one batch to the next may be a bit difficult, especially if you are mixing multiple dyes to create special colors. Since dyes are measured by weight, not volume, accurate mixing of custom colors requires the use of precision scales, which can be expensive. (However, if you are simply mixing a batch that will be used once, you can get away with using regular measuring spoons.)

The chemical properties that make dyes transparent also make them relatively sensitive to light. Unlike pigmented stains, which maintain their color, dyes will gradually fade when exposed to natural light. This lack of lightfastness is more of a problem with alcohol- and oil-soluble dyes than it is with water-soluble products.

Finally, as mentioned, dyes can be redissolved in the appropriate solvent even after they are dry. While this is helpful if you need to remove or correct the color of the dye, it may lead to other problems. Applying another coat of finish with the same solvent over a coat of dye will redissolve the dye and cause it to bleed into, or even through, the second coat of finish. This may not be too much of a concern if you are using spray equipment to apply the dye and topcoats, but it can cause headaches if you apply your finishes with a brush. If you try to brush a coat of clear water-based finish over a water-soluble dye, don't be surprised if you see the dye actually being lifted off the surface of the wood. The resulting finish may appear cloudy or muddy. Plus, the dye that is picked up and absorbed by the brush will be deposited in the can of finish, contaminating the clear topcoat.

Types of dyes

Dyes are classified according to the solvent in which the powder is dissolved. A dye may be water soluble, alcohol soluble, or oil soluble. The basic properties of the three types of dye stains are the same, and they are generally mixed, handled, and applied the same way. However, there are slight differences between the three products that give them each their own advantages as well as disadvantages.

WATER-SOLUBLE DYES

Water-soluble dyes offer the best lightfast properties, and they penetrate more deeply into the wood than alcohol- or oil-soluble dyes. Because the solvent is water, they are easy to mix, safe to use, and nonflammable. However, the water in the dye not only raises the grain of the wood but also makes these products the slowest drying of the three. This gives you more time to properly apply the dye, but it also means you have to wait longer for it to dry. However, even though water-soluble dyes dry slower in relation to their alcohol- and oil-soluble counterparts, they still dry much faster than oil-based pigmented stains.

ALCOHOL-SOLUBLE DYES

Alcohol-soluble dyes dry extremely fast and are good choices for touch-up work, tinting, and specialty applications such as shading and toning. Because they dry so fast, they can only be properly applied with a spray gun. You can try brushing them on, but you will most likely end up with lap marks. Most alcohol-soluble dyes have poor lightfast qualities. However, some manufacturers do offer alcohol-soluble dyes that have improved lightfastness. You will pay more for these dyes, but they probably still won't be as good at resisting fading as water-soluble dyes.

OIL-SOLUBLE DYES

Oil-soluble dyes are powders that can be dissolved in a variety of thinners. Mineral spirits, naphtha, turpentine, and kerosene may all be used, but these dyes are best dissolved in lacquer thinner. You may be using oil-soluble dyes in your shop and not even know it. Manufacturers often add these dyes to oil-based pigmented stains in an effort to help the stain color the wood more evenly. Adding oil-soluble dyes to pigmented stains also removes some of the dullness inherent in these products, giving the color a greater sense of brightness. Oil-soluble dyes are easier to use than alcohol-soluble products. They dry slowly enough to be applied with a brush and can be used to tint other oil-based finishes such as varnish and wiping oils. However, they lack the clarity of water-soluble dyes and, when used alone, may give the wood a dull, lifeless appearance.

Although you may find use for all three types of dye in your shop at one time or another, you will probably find water-soluble dyes to be the most practical and versatile and will end up using them significantly more than oil- or alcohol-soluble products. That, combined with the fact that the focus of this book is water-based finishes, means that I will now limit the discussion to mixing and using water-soluble dyes.

Mixing dyes

Mixing a batch of water-soluble dye is a fairly easy process. All you need is some clean water, a glass or plastic container, and the dye powder. Most manufacturers recommend that you use deionized water. Minerals that occur naturally in water may react with the dye, causing variations in color. However, I never seem to have a bottle of distilled water on hand when I need to mix a batch of dye, so I usually use plain old tap water. Although this may not be ideal, I have never noticed any ill effects.

It is also a good idea to mix the dye with warm or even hot water. Dye powders tend to clump and don't dissolve as well in cold water. Dissolving dyes in cold water requires more time, stirring, and patience, although I have often mixed dyes with cold water without any problems.

In addition to helping the powder dissolve better, warm water is thinner than cold water, which helps the dye penetrate more deeply into the wood. Whether you mix your dye with warm or

All you need to mix your own dyes are a rust-proof container, a few measuring devices, and some clean water.

When mixing dyes, always add the powder to the water. This not only helps the dye dissolve faster but also makes it easier to control the concentration of the solution.

cold water isn't as important as the temperature of the water when you apply the dye. If the dye is warm when you start finishing a piece and cools as you use it, the resulting color may be uneven. If possible, mix your dyes in advance and let them come to room temperature before applying them. By doing this, you will be assured of even penetration over the entire piece.

Mix the solution in a glass or plastic container. Metal cans may begin to oxidize, changing the color of the dye. I often use spaghetti sauce jars because they are the right size and readily available, but the metal lid eventually begins to rust and can be hard to open. For this reason, I prefer to use 1-quart plastic containers. They are easy to seal and reopen and have graduated

measurements on the side. However, if you use a lot of different colored dyes, stocking your shelves with these containers can get a bit expensive.

Once you have selected an appropriate container, fill it with the amount of water you will need to mix the dye. How much water you use depends on how strong you want the dye to be. Most manufacturers list the proper mixing ratio on the jar or package of dye. If you want the dye to be more concentrated or darker in color, use less water. Likewise, if you want the color to be weaker, increase the ratio of water to dye. Labeling your containers with the concentration of the mix is also a good idea.

Mix the dye slowly, adding a little powder at a time to the water and

Safety when using water-soluble dyes

One of the nice things about working with water-soluble dyes is they contain no smelly, toxic chemicals and are nonflammable. However, this does not mean you should not take some safety precautions. Although the commercially available dyes used by woodworkers no longer contain aniline, it is still not a good idea to breathe the powder or get the dye on your skin. Always wear a dust mask and rubber gloves when mixing and working with dyes.

Also, if you get any dye on your clothes, wash them separately. Once, after an especially long day of spraying more than 5 gallons of black dye, I threw my pants in the wash with a load of other clothes. Not only did the dye that washed out of my pants stain some of the other clothes but it also coated the inside of the washing machine and was picked up by the next load of laundry. Needless to say, I was not very popular around my house for a few days.

stirring thoroughly as you go. Once all the powder has been added, it is a good idea to let the mixture sit for a while before using it. If possible, I mix dyes the day before I plan to use them. This allows all of the powder to fully dissolve in the water. However, in a pinch I have used a dye 10 minutes after mixing it.

Regardless of how long you let the dye sit, always run it through a strainer if you apply it with a spray gun. No matter how well you mix it, there may still be small clumps of dye or other foreign particles that could clog the gun or spot the finish.

Applying dyes

The basic techniques and equipment used when applying dyes are no different from those used when working with pigmented stains. In general, the concept of flooding the surface and wiping off the excess does not change.

However, there are a few additional considerations to keep in mind when working with dyes.

First, test the color of the dye by applying some to a scrap piece of wood. When mixed in water, the dye may appear to be significantly different than the color of the dry powder. The way it looks when it is wet is how it will appear when the final topcoat is applied.

The beauty of water-soluble dyes is they can be applied in one of two ways. Either flood the surface with a brush, rag, or sponge and wipe off the excess before it dries, or build the color by brushing or spraying multiple light coats, letting each one dry undisturbed. The first technique is the easiest and leaves the least room for error. The second technique requires more practice and skill but when mastered is much quicker than the first. As a result, furniture manufacturers and production shops regularly color their pieces with the second method.

If you do decide to flood the surface and wipe off the excess, keep in mind that water-soluble dyes dry much faster than oil-based stains, so you should be prepared to work fairly quickly.

DEALING WITH RAISED GRAIN

As you are by now well aware, all water-based products have at least a slight tendency to raise grain. This is especially true with water-soluble dyes. Dyes are, after all, little more than colored water. They have no additives designed to speed up the drying process or limit grain raising. As a result, water-soluble dyes are perhaps the worst offenders when it comes to raising grain. Depending on your viewpoint, this may or may not be a problem. How you handle it is really a matter of individual preference.

Prewet and sand Perhaps the easiest and most obvious way to eliminate raised grain when using water-soluble dyes is to prewet and sand the wood prior to finishing. Simply raise the grain with water, then sand it off. If you do a good job, the grain will not raise any more, no matter how much dye or other water-based finish you apply. The trick is to do a thorough job of raising and sanding the grain before applying the dye. If you don't raise the grain enough, miss a spot, or do a poor job of sanding, you will be faced with more raised grain after the first coat of dye is applied. However, if you have never worked with dyes before, I would recommend this as the best way to eliminate raised grain.

Using the dye to raise the grain An alternative is to use the dye itself to raise the grain. Do this by applying a coat of dye just as you would water when prewetting and sanding. When the dye is dry, simply sand off the raised grain. This may seem like the easiest way to handle raised grain, since you are combining two steps into one. The problem is that when you sand off the raised grain, you will inevitably cut through the finish. If the raised grain is extremely bad, you may have to sand most of the dye off the surface. As a result, you will have to apply another coat of dye, which will change the depth and tone of the final color.

I do use this method on occasion but only when I know I will be applying two coats of dye anyway. I apply the first coat very lightly, sand off the raised grain, then use the second coat to develop the color I want.

Using sealers to stiffen the grain The final method, which is the one I use most frequently, involves the use of dyes and sealers to first raise, then stiffen the grain. Begin by applying a full coat of dye just as you would after wet sanding. When the dye is dry, the grain will be raised and feel quite rough. Next, brush or spray a thin coat of sealer over the surface. (For more on sealers, see Chapter 5.) I like to use a 1- or 2-pound cut of dewaxed shellac, but you can use any sealer you want.

The sealer serves two purposes. First, it stiffens the raised fibers, making them easy to sand, while greatly reducing the chances of cutting through the dye to bare wood. If you use a fine paper, such as 220 grit or even higher, and a light touch, you should be able to remove the raised grain to create a smooth surface without damaging or lightening the color of the dye. Second, the sealer has the added benefit of acting as a washcoat, sealing in the dye and preventing it from being redissolved or from bleeding through the next coat of finish.

When working with water-soluble dyes, this last method is my usual choice for dealing with raised grain. It greatly speeds the finishing process by turning what would be five steps into just three. Instead of raising the grain, sanding it, dying the wood, sealing the dye, and then sanding the sealer, now you simply dye the wood, seal it, and sand the sealer. In a production situation this proves to be a great time saver.

APPLICATION EQUIPMENT AND METHODS

Whether you flood the surface and wipe off the excess or apply multiple thin coats will depend both on your level of skill and the application equipment you choose. As with stains, dyes can be applied with rags, brushes, spray guns, sponges, pads, or rollers.

Rags When working with pigmented stains, rags are my choice for application. However, wiping dyes with rags may not always be the best method. A rag does a good job of flooding the surface with a lot of dye in a hurry, but I have found that because the dye is absorbed into the wood (unlike a pigmented stain that sits on the wood), the rag tends to drag over the surface. The grain that is raised by the dye snags the rag, picking up little pieces of lint while making the rag harder to move. On small projects this may not be a problem, but on large pieces like wall units and built-in cabinets, wiping on dye with a rag can be a tiring process.

If you do use a rag to wipe on the dye, simply dip the rag in the dye until it is saturated, then wipe it over the surface. Water-based dyes dry very evenly, so if you work quickly and keep the surface wet you won't have to worry about lap marks. In fact, you don't even have to worry about the direction in which you apply the dye. You can wipe the dye with the grain, against the grain, even in circles, as long as you apply it evenly over the entire surface.

One of the great things about dyes is that if you apply them carefully, you don't really need to go back and wipe the surface. Any thick spots will blend in and become virtually unnoticeable. However, once a piece is coated, it is still a good idea to go back over it with a clean cloth to remove any spills, drips, and puddles. If too much dye is left on the wood, it may dry before it can be absorbed, thus leaving behind a powder that may prevent the topcoat from adhering. Plus, with some dyes, a puddle or drip will absorb deeper into the wood and may, depending on the color of the dye, appear richer or darker. This can be a problem when using spray equipment, especially on areas where multiple passes overlap.

Brushes Although rags may not be the best tool to use for applying dyes, for my money brushes are even worse. While it is true that a brush creates less mess and gives you better control when reaching into tight areas, they are much slower to use. They may be fine for very small projects, but I generally avoid them when applying dye stains.

If you do decide to use a brush, be sure it is appropriate for the job. (For more on brush selection, see Chapter 7.) Choose a good-quality synthetic-bristle brush and be sure it is clean. If you use the same brush to apply other water-based products, anything left in the brush may redissolve and contaminate the finish.

Spray guns On larger projects I prefer to use a spray gun to apply dyes. They are faster and allow greater control of how much dye is applied to the surface. When using a spray gun, you should spray a full, wet, even coat over the entire piece. However, there are two different ways to achieve the same results.

The first, and probably easier, way to apply dye with a spray gun is to use it just as you would a rag. Spray a thick, wet coat over the entire piece, then use a clean cloth to wipe off any excess, puddles, drips, and runs. The dye goes on much quicker than it would with a rag, thus giving you plenty of time to wipe the piece dry. This is fine for one piece of furniture, and I often use this method in my shop.

When faced with a larger project such as a library full of cabinets or 2,000 ft. of molding, I employ another method, which may seem like more work but is much faster and less tiring in the long run.

This method of application uses the spray gun to control how thick the coat of dye goes on and hence its color. Rather than flooding the surface with a wet coat that must then be wiped dry, I apply a much lighter coat that dries fairly quickly. When the first coat is dry, I spray a second coat to deepen and even out the color.

How, you may ask, is spraying two coats quicker than spraying just one? It isn't. The time is saved by eliminating the wiping and handling of each piece. It is much quicker and easier to spray something than it is to wipe it with a rag. Often I will spray a light coat on a large piece and immediately spray a second coat before setting it aside to dry. The piece only has to be handled once and it is done.

The drawback to this method is that it takes a lot of practice. Controlling the color by how heavy you spray the dye takes some getting used to and can be difficult. This is especially true in areas where the dye tends to go on heavier, such as where spray passes overlap. I always keep a clean rag on hand just in case I need to give a quick wipe to remove a drip or puddle of dye.

Sponges, foam brushes, pads, and rollers As with pigmented stains, dyes can be applied with sponges, foam brushes, pads, and rollers. However, they all have their limitations. Because water-soluble dyes raise the grain of the wood, the rough surface will eat into a sponge or foam pad. For this reason, I only recommend using them on small projects.

I can't imagine applying dye on an area that is so large that you would need a pad applicator or roller. Generally these are used when staining large areas like floors or paneled walls. Because dyes are not as lightfast as pigmented stains, you would not be using them on projects of this nature.

Dense woods like hard maple can be difficult to dye. The right half of this board was misted with water a few minutes before the dye was applied. The water primed the wood by opening the pores. The resulting finish is less blotchy and appears deeper and clearer.

CONTROLLING COLOR

No matter which application method you use, the key to working with water-soluble dyes lies in your ability to control the final color. How you do this depends on both the concentration of the dye and how it is applied to the wood.

The first step in controlling color begins with how the dye is mixed. The higher the ratio of dye to solvent, the darker the color will be. I start by using less water than the manufacturer recommends, then I adjust the color from there. For example, if the directions say to mix an ounce of powder in a quart of water, I may start by mixing an ounce of dye in a pint of water. From there I gradually add more water until I have the shade I want.

Dyes also give you the luxury of adjusting the color after they are applied. For example, if the first coat of dye is too light, simply let it dry and apply another coat. Or you can apply a heavy coat of dye without removing the excess. If, on

Dense woods also absorb dyes better if they are not sanded too finely. The left half of this piece of maple was sanded to 120 grit, while the right half was sanded to 180 grit. Notice how the left side absorbs the dye more evenly and appears less blotchy.

the other hand, the dye you've just applied is too dark, wipe the surface with a damp cloth. The water will redissolve the dye, allowing it to be removed from the surface. Although you may need to

As dyes dry, they become dull and hazy. Compare the dry dye on the left with the wet dye on the right. Although they are the same color, the wet dye looks deeper, richer, shinier, and more alive.

use bleach to remove all of the color, in most cases you will be able to significantly lighten the dye without it.

Because dyes color evenly, they are a good choice for hard-to-stain woods such as pine and cherry. But not even dyes are exempt from occasional blotching and absorption problems on tight-pored, dense woods such as hard maple. To avoid blotchiness on these woods, I often mist the surface with water a few minutes before applying the dye. The water acts as a primer to open the pores of the wood, allowing it to absorb more dye. The resulting finish is deeper and has a brighter look.

Don't be concerned when a freshly applied coat of dye begins to dry. When the dye first goes on, it will appear wet, shiny, and have a deep, rich tone. However, after it has dried for a few minutes, it will appear dull and lifeless and may even develop a white haze over the surface. Don't panic though, since the dye will return to its original appearance once a clear topcoat is applied. In most cases, you can assume that the way a dye looks immediately after it is applied will be how it will look when your project is finished.

Nongrain-raising (NGR) dyes

In addition to water-based pigmented stains and water-soluble dyes, there is a third choice to consider when coloring the wood. Nongrain-raising (NGR) dyes are water-soluble dyes that have fast-drying alcohols added to them. For the most part, they look, act, and are applied just like water-soluble dyes, but they dry even faster. The concept behind them is that the alcohol, by replacing some of the water, limits the amount of and time that water is sitting on the wood. In theory,

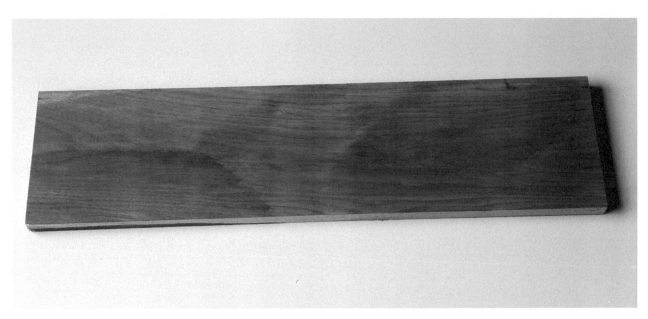

Because NGR dyes dry so fast, they tend to show lap marks more than water-soluble dyes. They also appear a bit muddier, as evidenced by the somewhat obscured grain in this piece of butternut.

this should, as their name implies, eliminate the amount of grain that is raised by the dye. Although some manufacturers claim their NGR dyes will not raise the grain, I have not found this to be entirely true. In my experience, NGR dyes will raise the grain a slight amount.

NGR dyes do have some advantages over regular water-soluble dyes. First, because they are premixed, you don't have to worry about measuring, mixing, and straining. Second, factory-mixed NGR dyes will be somewhat more consistent in color from one batch to the next than dyes you mix yourself.

NGR dyes do contain a few disadvantages though. The additives make them more dangerous and certainly more flammable than water-soluble dyes. In my mind, this defeats one of the reasons for using water-soluble products in the first place. NGR

dyes are also more difficult to use than water-soluble dyes. Because NGR dyes dry so fast, you don't really have enough time to wipe off any excess. As a result, they tend to show lap marks. For this reason, they are best applied with a spray gun, using multiple light coats to build color.

NGR dyes also lack the clarity and brightness of water-soluble dyes. In fact, they often appear dull, cloudy, or even muddy. Plus, a quart of NGR dye costs more than a comparable package of water-soluble powder.

Because of their minimal grain raising and the speed at which they dry, NGR dyes are most often used by larger furniture manufacturers and production shops. Although I do use them occasionally, when given the choice I will always opt for water-soluble dyes. Their ease of use and versatility can't be beat.

7

Clear Topcoats

Whether you stain, dye, or want to keep the wood's natural color, you will no doubt want to protect the surface of the wood with a clear topcoat. But clear finishes do a lot more than simply protect the wood. When applied properly, the right finish can give the surface a warm, soft glow or a hard, high shine. Clear topcoats also add a sense of depth to the wood. The key is in selecting the right product for the job at hand. Just as one coat of sanding sealer would not be a suitable finish for a chair or table, several coats of expensive urethane floor finish on the inside of a drawer would be overkill.

Since some water-based finishes do certain things better than others, which finish to use depends not on what it is called but how it performs. Ultimately, the choice is a matter of personal preference. I have tried numerous products in my shop but always turn to the same two or three brands for all of my finishing work. While there are other products that will work as well, I am comfortable with a few specific brands so I stick with them.

No matter what finish you use, the first thing you need is a clean, warm area to apply the finish. If you are brushing a water-based finish, this could be a garage, basement, or just about any room in your house. If you are spraying the finish, you should have an area that is well ventilated. Because these finishes are nonflammable, you do not need a professional spray booth. However, you do need a well-ventilated area and should always wear a particle mask or respirator.

Once you have chosen your finishing area, it is important to properly prepare the finish before applying it. The next crucial step is knowing how to apply the finish, whether you are brushing or spraying. Finally, a good sanding job is necessary for success.

Application equipment

All finishes that can be applied with a brush can also be sprayed. However, there are some water-based finishes that are designed for spraying only. The application equipment you choose depends on several factors, including the type of finish, the equipment you have available, and the size of the project. Although I like to spray finish whenever possible, on smaller projects I often use a brush. Whether you choose to brush or spray your finishes, the important thing is to begin with the proper equipment.

BRUSHES

The first step to success when working with water-based finishes lies in the brush you choose. The wrong brush will be difficult to use, won't allow you to flow on much material, and will lose its shape, leaving brush and lap marks on the surface. The right brush will flow a large amount of finish on the surface quickly and easily, will hold its shape, and won't mar the finish or cause streaking.

While it is true that you get what you pay for, simply buying the most expensive brush won't guarantee good results. Typically, the more expensive brushes are those that contain natural bristles. These brushes are great for applying oil-based products and shellac, but they aren't very good for water-based finishes. Natural bristles absorb a great deal of water. (In some cases, they may absorb as much as 100% of their weight in water.) As they absorb the water in the finish, they tend to become soft or limp and will eventually droop and lose their shape. The brush's ability to flow a smooth coat over the surface of

Natural-bristle brushes will absorb water to the point where they lose their shape and become difficult to use.

the wood will be greatly diminished and the floppy bristles will leave marks all over the finish. Because the natural bristles absorb some of the finish, these brushes are also difficult to clean.

The best brush to use when working with water-based products is one with a synthetic bristle. Synthetic-bristle brushes vary tremendously in quality, price, and performance. Good-quality synthetic-bristle brushes contain man-made filaments that closely resemble natural bristles. They hold a good amount of finish and are firm enough to maintain their shape but not so stiff that they are difficult to use or leave ugly streaks in the finish. An inexpensive synthetic brush, on the other hand, will not hold much liquid and will not flow on the finish as well. However, an inexpensive synthetic-bristle brush is still better for applying water-based products

A chisel-cut brush (left) has bristles that taper to a slightly rounded point in the middle. A square- or flat-edge brush (right) has bristles that are all the same length.

than an expensive natural-bristle brush. Synthetic bristles absorb very little water and therefore do not become floppy or lose their shape. This not only makes them easier to use than natural-bristle brushes but also easier to clean.

There are a few things to look for when selecting a synthetic-bristle brush. The most important is the type of bristle itself. A good-quality synthetic brush will look and feel very much like a natural-bristle brush. The bristles should be stiff enough to handle relatively thick water-based coatings but not so stiff that they are difficult to bend or flex. The ends of the bristles may be cut square, tapered to a point, or split into smaller strands. The square-, or blunt-, cut brushes are good for painting but are not the best choice for finishing furniture. Tapered bristles

are thicker near the handle and thinner at the ends. Thinner ends mean more bristles come in contact with the workpiece, which in turn means the finish is spread more evenly. Bristles that have split, or flagged, tips hold more material and do the best job of spreading the finish evenly.

The way the bristles are cut in relation to one another is important as well. Some brushes, called square- or flat-edged brushes, have bristles that are all the same length. Chisel-edged brushes have bristles that taper in length from the middle of the brush to the outside edges. Although both types of brushes will work with water-based products, chisel-edged brushes are better for controlling how the finish is applied and smoothed out.

With all these options, the obvious question is what type of brush is best for applying water-based finishes on fine furniture. When buying a brush, I look for a good-quality synthetic bristle with tapered or flagged ends that are chisel cut. If you had to own only one brush, a 2-in. width is probably the most versatile. It holds enough liquid and is large enough to coat big areas but is not so big that you can't use it for smaller objects and more detailed work.

SPRAY GUNS

There is no question that using a spray gun is my favorite way to apply water-based products. The finish goes on easily, flows out and levels nicely, and dries fast. Best of all, you don't have to worry about large air bubbles, lap marks, or the possibility of the previous coat of finish being lifted off the surface. However, if you do plan to use spray

Nothing beats a spray gun for production work. Imagine how long it would take to paint all these boxes by hand.

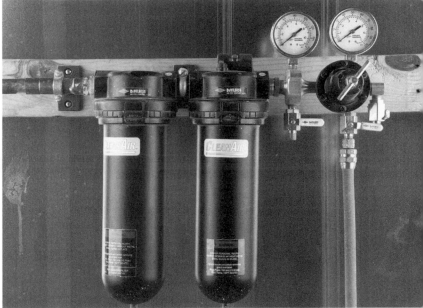

A good-quality air-filtration system, such as this one showing a separator (left) and coalescer (right), is essential when spraying with compressed air.

equipment to apply water-based products, there are, naturally, a few things to consider.

To begin with, water will corrode metal, so ideally the parts of the gun that come in contact with the finish should be stainless steel or plastic. However, if your gun is not water-resistant, you do not have to run out and buy a new one. I regularly spray water-based finishes through a gun that is not stainless steel. The way to keep it from corroding is to be sure it is thoroughly dry at the end of each use. The easiest way to do this is by drying off the gun with compressed air. If you are using a turbine-driven system and do not have an air compressor, simply run a few ounces of denatured alcohol through the system as the last step in the cleaning process. The alcohol will remove any remaining

water and help keep the gun dry and corrosion free.

Water-based products are delicate mixes that must be kept in balance. They are especially sensitive to contaminants like dirt, grease, oil, and dirty water, so it is important that your gun and air supply are as clean as possible. (For more on cleaning spray equipment, see Chapter 10.) Of course, the more you spend on a filtration system, the cleaner your air will be. At the very least, you should have a separator that will remove dirt and water from the compressed air. If you want an even cleaner air supply, install a coalescer after the separator. A coalescer removes even smaller particles by passing the air through a glass fiber filter. If you really want pure air, you could also install a dryer between the coalescer and the gun that will remove

Disposable in-line filters are less expensive alternatives to fixed filters and come in handy when spraying at a job site.

Turbines keep your air system clean and are easy to maintain. Just clean or change the filter from time to time.

any remaining moisture from the air. If your budget won't allow for expensive filters, you should at least install an in-line filter as close to the gun as possible. These filters are designed to be used a few times then thrown away. They are inexpensive, easy to install, and do a passable job of removing impurities from the air supply.

If your spray system runs off a turbine, keeping the air supply clean is a much easier task. All you really need to do to maintain a turbine is to keep the air filter clean.

Turbine-driven systems By far the cheapest and easiest spray system to buy and set up in the average small shop is a turbine-driven high-volume, low-pressure (HVLP) system. These systems consist of an HVLP gun that uses a large volume of slow-moving air to atomize the finish material. The gun is attached to a turbine, which provides air flow. A turbine is little more than a vacuum cleaner motor in a box. Fans, or stages, compress the air and move it through a large-diameter hose to the gun.

The beauty of turbine-driven systems is they are compact, inexpensive, and portable. The drawback is they are limited in the amount of air pressure they are capable of delivering to the tip of the gun. A typical three-stage turbine, which is probably the most common unit you will find in a small shop, delivers at most 6 psi to the tip of the gun. While this is plenty of pressure to atomize most coatings, it may not be enough for some heavy fluids. The high solids content typical of most water-based products makes them relatively thick, or high in viscosity. The higher the viscosity of a product, the more air

Adjusting viscosity for better spraying

Viscosity tells us how thick, or thin, a liquid is. It is a measurement of a liquid's resistance to flow. Put another way, viscosity is a measurement of the amount of friction between the molecules of finish. It tells us how easily those molecules slide past each other. This may sound great if you have a chemistry lab and a microscope. But what exactly does this mean for the average finisher?

The viscosity of a finish really isn't that important if you use brushes to apply your finishes. However, if you use spray equipment, understanding what viscosity is and how to measure it plays a much more critical role. Different factors determine how much air comes from the tip of a gun. The size of the compressor or turbine, the diameter of the air hose, and the size and configuration of the air cap and the passages in the gun all combine to determine exactly what the air pressure at the tip of the gun is or can be. If the air pressure is not great enough, the fluid will not atomize properly. The resulting drops of finish will be so large that they can't flow together properly and will form a rough, textured surface that resembles the skin of an orange (appropriately called orange peel). Likewise, if the pressure at the tip of the gun is too great for the material being sprayed, it will break into particles that are so small that they dry before hitting the surface being finished. This "dry spray" will also be rough but will appear more like sandpaper than citrus fruit.

It probably sounds like the air pressure at the tip of the gun is what is really important, not the viscosity of the fluid. If the finish won't flow properly, simply adjust the gun, right? Well, to a certain degree that is correct. The problem is that adjusting the air pressure at the tip of the gun is not always easy to do. With some guns you may be able to increase or decrease the pressure simply by changing the air cap. With other guns you may have to change the air cap and a baffle system that contains rings and gaskets. This means every time you change finish materials you have to take your gun apart and change components. Plus, what do you do when you need to raise the psi at the tip of the gun but can't?

The answer is simple: Rather than trying to adjust your gun, adjust the fluid. If the gun can't generate enough air pressure to atomize a thick fluid, simply make the fluid thinner. This is where the measurement of viscosity comes in.

First, you need some way of knowing how thick the fluid should be to spray properly, then you have to have a way to accurately and consistently thin the fluid to the right consistency. Fortunately, finish manufacturers make the first part easy by telling us what the viscosity of their finishes should be for proper spraying. For example, the label may say "23 seconds in #2 Zahn cup." What this means is that when a #2 Zahn viscosity cup is filled, it should take 23 seconds for it to empty.

Once you know this, thinning the material to the right viscosity is a simple matter of trial and error. Add a little thinner, check the viscosity, and then, if needed, add a little more. Once you know how much thinner you need to add to get the finish to the right viscosity, you will be able to thin a new batch any time with similar results.

Viscosity-Cup Conversion Chart

Don't worry if the viscosity cup you have is a different brand or number than the one specified on the can of finish. This conversion chart makes it easy to interchange cups.

Zahn #1	Zahn #2	Fischer #1	Fischer #2	Ford Cup #3	Ford Cup #4
30	16	20			5
34	17	25			8
37	18	30	15	12	10
41	19	35	17	15	12
44	20	39	18	19	14
52	22	50	21	25	18
60	24		24	29	22
68	27		29	33	25
	30		33	36	28
	34		39	41	31
	37		44	45	32
	41		50	50	34
	49		62	58	41
	58			66	45
	66				50
	74				54
	82				58

The numbers in this chart refer to the time in seconds it takes the cup to empty.

pressure is needed to obtain proper atomization. In particular, extremely high-solids coatings like pigmented primers may be too thick to spray without thinning.

Compressed-air systems The first spray equipment I owned was a turbine-driven HVLP system. A few years later, I invested in a large air compressor and a compressed-air HVLP gun. Since then, I can count the number of times I have used the turbine-driven system on one hand. There is nothing wrong with turbines; I have simply found that when it comes to spraying water-based finishes in a production situation, nothing beats a compressed-air HVLP system.

While there are many reasons for using compressed air to spray finish, the main one is that you have infinitely better control over how much air is delivered to the tip of the gun. While this may not be of prime importance when spraying light-bodied materials like nitrocellulose lacquer, it is a major consideration when working with relatively thick finishes. For example, when using my turbine-driven system to spray water-based finishes, I regularly have to add thinner to achieve proper atomization. With my compressed-air system, I spray the same materials without a drop of thinner. In fact, the only product I ever need to thin before spraying is a very thick pigmented primer.

If you do decide to use compressed air to spray water-based finishes, be sure your gun is clean. In particular, be careful if you use the same gun to spray solvent-based products as well. Water-based finishes will loosen dried particles of solvent-based finishes that may be stuck in the gun. The little clumps will then become trapped in your clear water-based topcoats. They will spot the finish and may require a significant amount of sanding to remove.

Any spray gun will work with water-based products, but some are better than others. After trying several different guns, I have recently settled on one that was designed specifically for water-based finishes. It requires less air pressure to operate and, due to the design of the baffle and air cap, emits a relatively soft spray.

Safety equipment

Even though water-based finishes are nontoxic and relatively safe compared to solvent-based products, they still contain chemicals and resins that may be harmful. This is not really a problem when applying them with a brush. However, spray guns atomize the finish into tiny particles and spread them throughout the air. Even if you have good air circulation or a professional spray booth, you are bound to breathe in some of the overspray that comes from even the best HVLP equipment. For this reason, you should always wear a vapor respirator. Some manufacturers of water-based products say you only need to wear a particle filter or dust mask when spraying their finishes, but I have always felt safer wearing a charcoal-filter respirator.

If you do a lot of spraying, you should also take precautions to keep overspray off your skin. Prolonged exposure to anything can be bad for you, so it makes sense to limit your contact with these finishes by wearing appropriate clothing and, if necessary, gloves.

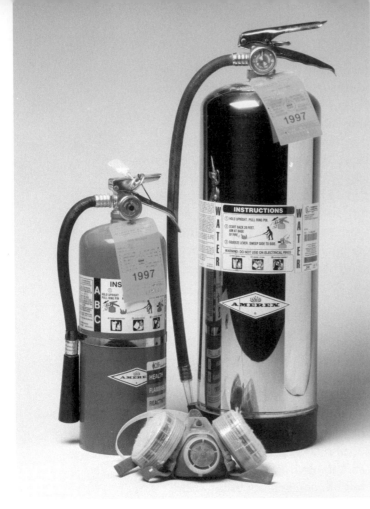

A good vapor mask and at least one fire extinguisher should be standard equipment in any finishing room.

One final piece of safety equipment that should be a part of any shop is a fire extinguisher. It may seem unnecessary to have one on hand when using water-based finishes since they are nonflammable. However, even if the only finishes you use are water based, you will no doubt have cans of various solvent-based products like acetone, lacquer thinner, mineral spirits, and alcohol lying around your shop. Many of these are explosive, so it makes sense to have at least one fire extinguisher on hand.

Application conditions

Water-based finishes are without a doubt more sensitive to their surroundings than are most other finishes. If the weather is warm and dry, they are very easy to work with. However, if it is cold or humid, they become problematic. If you think about it, this makes sense. Water-based finishes dry as the water in the solution evaporates. If the air is warm and dry, water will evaporate rather quickly. If the air is cold or contains a lot of moisture, water will evaporate much more slowly.

Under ideal conditions, which are generally described as 70°F with relative humidity ranging from 30% to 50%, water-based finishes are easy to spray or brush, flow out well, and dry quickly. On a dry summer day, you should have no problem applying one coat every couple of hours. If you are fortunate enough to live in a part of the country that is warm and dry all year, consider yourself lucky. The rest of us must deal with hot, wet summers and freezing cold winters. Applying water-based finishes under these conditions becomes a bit more challenging.

HUMIDITY
When the humidity is high, the drying time for a water-based product may increase significantly. On a hot, sticky summer day when the humidity is near 100%, a finish that would normally be dry enough to touch in 5 minutes may still be tacky after 30 minutes. Likewise, the time you must allow before sanding may be doubled, tripled, or even quadrupled. This not only slows down the finishing process but also allows greater opportunity for dust to settle into the wet finish.

This does not mean that you cannot apply water-based finishes on humid days. I do it all the time. In fact, whenever I have a project that needs to be done in a hurry, the one thing I can count on is that it will start raining. Although you could use dehumidifiers to lessen or even eliminate the effects of humidity in your shop, I suspect that for most people this is not a realistic option. While large furniture manufacturers can afford expensive exhaust systems that keep the air dry, the rest of us must deal with humidity the best we can.

There are two ways to combat the effects of humidity. First, apply slightly thinner coats than you would normally. A thinner coat will naturally dry faster than a thick one. Second, have a steady supply of air moving through the room to help the finish dry more quickly. An extra fan placed a few feet from the finished piece will greatly reduce the time it takes to dry. (Just be careful you're not blowing dust all over the place.) Although you may never be able to completely eliminate the effect humidity has on a water-based finish, you should be able to control it enough to make it tolerable.

TEMPERATURE

Unfortunately, water-based products react to cold weather even worse than they do to humidity. Fortunately, cold weather is a much easier problem to solve: Simply turn up the heat, right? That sounds great to those of us who have heated shops, but what about someone who is working in a cold garage or unheated barn? Well, I hate to say it, but if you can't raise the temperature beyond a certain point, you are out of luck. Water-based products have what is known as a "minimum film-forming temperature," below which they will not dry properly. This temperature may vary slightly for different products, but in general it is around 50°. If the temperature of the air, the piece being finished, or the finish itself is below this point, the finish won't work. The finish may not flow or level properly, adhesion may be a problem, it may never dry, or water may become trapped in the finish, casting a blue haze over the entire piece. (Someone once told me he put a heavy coat of finish on a project in a cold barn in the middle of the winter. When he came back the next day the finish had turned purple!) In short, if you work in an unheated shop, you may have to consider using a different finish or moving your finishing room indoors.

If your shop is heated, you may still have problems with cold air. Even with the heat on, shops with high ceilings and concrete floors stay cold in the winter. At least three different cabinetmakers have told me they don't use water-based products specifically because they are afraid of what will happen when the weather gets cold. They all think that if you don't keep your heat set to a comfortable 70°, you can't use these finishes. This is simply not true. I used to work in a finishing room that had a huge, open fan in the exterior wall of the shop. The room had no heat and had to be warmed by turning on the fan and pulling warm air in from the body of the shop. Needless to say, the room got pretty cold in the winter. But even so, I regularly sprayed water-based products regardless of the outside temperature.

There are a number of things you can do if you want to apply water-based finishes in a cold room. The first, and most obvious, is to make sure the piece being finished is relatively warm. Next,

Turbines and hot air

Some people may tell you that the warm, dry air generated by turbines is good for the finish. There is no question that dry air is a requirement for successful spraying. However, saying that warm air is good for the finish simply is not true. In fact, the warm (and sometimes even hot) air coming from a turbine may impede the ability of a finish to flow out and level by flashing off some of the solvents at the tip of the gun. In effect, the finish has begun drying before it even hits the target and may not flow together properly. The best way to help a finish on a cold day is to heat the *finish*, not the air used to apply it.

introduce some heat to the room. This does not mean you have to make it warm enough to walk around in shorts, but you should try to take the chill out of the air. I regularly sprayed when the temperature in the finishing room wasn't much over 50°. Although the finish took a bit longer than normal to dry, it flowed out and leveled fine.

If the room is really cold and you simply can't (or can't afford) to heat it beyond a certain point, the next thing to try is warming the finish itself. To do this, place the can of finish in a large container that is filled with hot water. The finish will absorb the heat from the water and warm up in 5 to 10 minutes. Warm finish is a joy to apply. For lack of a better word, it feels "lighter" and flows out to a smooth, dry coat much more quickly than cold finish will.

Finally, if the finish does not dry properly because the air is too cold, try introducing heat into the drying process. Placing a fan behind an electric heater is one way to move warm air over a drying project. Another way is to use a heat lamp. When I need to dry something in a hurry on a cold day, I often train a halogen work light directly toward the project. These lights generate enough heat so that the finish is dry enough to sand in an hour or two. Remember that you are only trying to speed up the drying process, not bake on the finish. You don't have to leave the heat source on all day.

Material preparation

One of the keys to success when using water-based topcoats is how well the material is prepared prior to application. Water-based topcoats are complex formulations of several chemicals, resins, and additives. As a result, they must be treated a little more carefully than traditional solvent-based products. Danish oils and solvent-based varnishes generally need little or no preparation prior to use. Simply stir them and begin finishing. Water-based products, on the other hand, require a bit more care, especially if you are using spray equipment.

STIRRING

Shaking a can of water-based finish can be the kiss of death for a clear topcoat, especially if you are applying it with a brush. The low surface tension of the surfactant-laced water found in these finishes will cause the material to foam and bubble with even the slightest bit of agitation. If you are running your finish through a spray gun, you probably won't have too many problems. However, if you are using a brush, even the slightest sign of bubbling or foaming is a cause for concern. No matter how careful you are with the brush, the bubbles created by shaking the can prior to use will find their way into the finish.

The results usually aren't pretty—the bubbles will remain in the film as it dries, leaving behind ugly bumps, air pockets, and spots that can only be removed by thorough, time-consuming sanding. In severe cases, you will have to remove the entire coat and begin again. The easiest way to avoid bubbles in the finish is to agitate the can as little as possible prior to use. You should stir the material gently yet thoroughly with a clean stick.

THINNING

Unlike nitrocellulose lacquer and shellac, which can be thinned to no end, water-based products don't like to be thinned. Adding thinner to an already delicate mix can greatly upset the balance of the finish and create all sorts of problems. Water-based products have a high solids content. If the finish is too thin, the solids will begin to sag and drip. The material may lose its ability to cling to vertical surfaces and run. Likewise, a thin finish may dry too fast to be brushed, or when sprayed it may turn to powder before it hits the target.

Although it is best to avoid adding thinners to most water-based products, there are times when you will need to add a little thinner. For example, I use a pigmented primer that is so thick I couldn't possibly spray it straight from the can. In this case, I thin the primer by about 5% until it is the right viscosity for spraying.

The question when thinning these products is what thinner to use. Some manufacturers state that their products should never be thinned. Others may say its okay to thin them but only with their special flow additives. Still others tell you that if necessary, thin with water. With most finishes, water is an acceptable thinner. Flow additives are really nothing more than water with some alcohol

Additives for water-based products include extender (left), which is used to lengthen the "open" time of brushable finishes; flow additive (center); and paint conditioner (right), which helps latex paint flow and level better.

Strainers come in a variety of shapes and sizes. They all do the same thing, so which you choose is a matter of availability and personal preference.

added. The water thins the finish while the alcohol slows down the drying time enough to allow the finish to flow out and level. Extenders are similar to flow additives in that they contain water, which thins the finish, and various alcohols. These alcohols control the rate at which water evaporates out of the finish. The slower drying the alcohol, the longer the finish will stay wet, or open. Extenders are useful if you want to brush a finish that is primarily designed to be sprayed, and they also come in handy if you live in a particularly warm, dry climate like the Southwest.

If you must thin the material, do so carefully. Begin by adding small amounts of water or flow additive until you reach the desired viscosity. It is also important to stir the finish well, otherwise the thinner may simply float on top. Most manufacturers will tell you how much their finish can be thinned. If you have to add more than the recommended

thinner to get the material to spray properly, your spray system is underpowered and you should probably consider switching to another finish material or application method.

STRAINING

If you use a brush to apply water-based finishes, you shouldn't need to strain them. However, if you use a spray gun, straining is a must. When it comes to small particles and clumps in the finish, water-based products are like magnets. It is not unusual for dried finish to collect around the rim and sides of the can. This becomes more of a problem the older the finish gets. When you open the lid and stir the finish, particles break off and fall in. Even a tiny lump may be enough to clog a spray gun. If a lump of dried finish does become stuck in the gun, you must remove the finish from the cup or pressure pot and clean the entire system thoroughly before straining the finish back into the material container and starting over again. Having to stop in the middle of a job and go through the cleaning process is frustrating and time consuming. The few minutes spent running the finish through a strainer are well worth it.

It is also important to strain heavy-bodied materials like pigmented primers. The high solids content of these products causes them to congeal and clump quickly. Pigmented primers are so thick that it may seem like it takes forever to run them through a strainer. If you're in a hurry, add thinner to the primer first to greatly reduce the amount of straining time.

It doesn't really matter what type of strainer you use as long as the holes are big enough to let the finish flow through but small enough to catch foreign particles. When filling a 1-quart cup, I like to use round plastic strainers. They fit into the opening of the cup nicely and are easy to keep clean. Paper filters are cheap and disposable, but they tend to be a bit flimsy and messy to use. When filling a pressure pot, I prefer nylon mesh filters. These large, sack-like strainers fit easily over the opening of the pot, strain a lot of material quickly, and are easy to clean and reuse. If kept clean, a nylon filter should last for years.

Brushing techniques

I don't think I know a person who has not had some experience brushing a coat of paint on the side of a house or a piece of interior trim. But applying finishes on furniture involves a lot more than simply dipping the brush in the can and slapping on the coating. In fact, good brushing technique is critical to a good finish.

Before you even pick up a brush, you should be sure you are using the right finish. Some water-based products are designed for production work and are meant to be applied with spray equipment. Although you could use a brush, they dry so fast that the results would be disappointing. The best way to be sure your finish is meant for brushing is to read the label. Most manufacturers list appropriate application equipment on the can.

Before you begin brushing, make sure your brush is clean. Dried finish tends to accumulate between the bristles, especially near the handle. If you use a brush that has not been well cleaned, the old finish will crack and loosen, falling into your nice wet finish. Before you use

any brush, you should flex the bristles a few times, then tap them firmly against the palm of your hand. This should loosen any old finish, dirt, or broken bristles. Before dipping the brush into the finish, wet it all the way up to the ferrule with the appropriate solvent. (For water-based finishes, use water; for shellac, use alcohol.) This will not only help prime the brush for the finish but will also make it much easier to clean later.

When you first open a can of water-based finish, don't be surprised by the color of the liquid. Unlike solvent-based finishes, which are usually fairly clear, water-based products appear cloudy or milky. The resins used in water-based finishes appear cloudy when suspended in a liquid state, but they clear up as the finish dries. Unless you plan to use an entire can of finish on one job, pour what you need into a separate, clean

Compared with the clear, solvent-based product shown on the left, cans of water-based finish appear white or milky.

container. This will prevent any contaminants that may be picked up by the brush from becoming mixed with the rest of the finish.

Begin brushing by dipping your brush one-third to one-half of the way into the finish and pulling it out slowly. Because water-based finishes tend to bubble and foam easily, it is important that you don't agitate the material with the brush any more than you have to. Above all, resist the temptation to drag the wet brush across the edge of the container to remove excess liquid. Instead, hold the brush over the can and let the finish run off by itself. When most of it has drained off, tap the side of the brush against the inside edge of the can to remove any remaining drops that may otherwise fall off the brush onto the piece being finished. This may seem like a slow way to load the brush, but it is better to take

Instead of dragging a finish-filled brush across the rim of the can, hold it above the container and let the excess run off the brush naturally. This greatly reduces the amount of bubbles in the finish.

If your finish bubbles and foams despite your efforts to be careful, you can try further reducing the surface tension of the material by adding a few drops of milk, mineral spirits, or lacquer thinner.

the extra few seconds here to avoid creating bubbles than it is to have to sand dried bubbles out of the finish.

The key to success when brushing water-based materials lies in how well you flow the material onto the wood. Ideally you want to lay down a full, wet coat using the fewest brushstrokes possible. The more you work the finish, the greater the chance that it will develop bubbles. In addition, because these finishes dry quickly, too much brushing may not only leave brush marks or streaks but may also lift partially dry finish off the surface. Think of the brush as being less a brush in the traditional sense and more like a squeegee.

Begin your first stroke a few inches from the edge of a piece and, holding the brush at a comfortable angle, make a long, smooth stroke. Then go back to where you started and finish the stroke in the other direction, off the edge of the wood. Working from the inside of the board toward the edge will greatly eliminate the chance of finish scraping off the brush and running down the side of the wood.

Make your next pass parallel to the first, overlapping an inch or so. The best way to avoid lap marks is by always working from a wet edge. If you work quickly enough, you shouldn't have any trouble doing this.

Once you have coated an area, you may want to go back and lightly smooth out the surface. Hold the brush nearly perpendicular to the work piece and make a series of quick, very light passes, being sure that only the tips of the bristles come in contact with the wood. This process, known as tipping off, works well with slow-drying finishes but can be difficult to do with water-based

Holding your brush at a 30° to 45° angle, start a few inches in from the end of the piece and take a long, fluid stroke (top). Then go back and finish the stroke in the opposite direction (bottom).

Brushes: A word of caution

The first time I brushed a clear water-based finish over a water-soluble dye I was surprised to find that each time I dipped the brush into the finish, some type of dirty brown material would be left behind. At first I was confused, but I quickly came to the conclusion that the brush must have been contaminated with an oil-based product. I switched to another brush, but the same thing happened. Was it possible that all of my brushes were dirty?

After promising myself that I would from that day forward do a better job of cleaning my equipment, I reached for a brush that had never been used. This one, I was sure, couldn't possibly be contaminated with anything. Imagine my surprise when the brand-new brush dripped the same brown liquid back into the can of finish! Fortunately, it didn't

take me long to figure out where the mysterious contaminant was coming from. When I stepped back and really looked at the brown material mixed in with the clear finish, I realized it was pretty much the same color as the dye. Therein was the answer.

As mentioned, water-soluble dyes are easily redissolved when coated with water. As the water in the clear finish dissolved the dye, the brush began to pick it up and move it around the surface. Each time I dipped the brush in the can, some of the dye was left floating in the clear topcoat. The

resulting finish was a little uneven in color, mottled, and cloudy.

Does this mean you can't brush water-based finishes over water-soluble dyes? Certainly not, as long as you seal the dye first. While you could brush on a coat of water-based sealer, that would probably cause the same problem. Instead, apply a coat of dewaxed shellac in a 1- or 2-pound cut. Since the shellac is alcohol based, it won't disturb the dye. The dye will be sealed beneath the shellac and the resulting surface will be uniform in color and easy to sand.

When brushing topcoats over dyes, it is a good idea to seal the dye first, otherwise the brush may lift the color off the surface and deposit it in the clear finish.

products. If the surface is still wet, tipping it off will remove air bubbles and brush and lap marks. However, if the surface has begun to dry, tipping it off will create more problems than it solves. The bristles will dig into the film and leave visible marks and may even scrape some of the finish off the surface. Under the right conditions, most water-based products do a good job of leveling out after they have been applied. The best advice I could give anyone who is brushing on a water-based product for the first time would be to apply the finish and leave it alone. The more you "worry" it with a brush, the worse it will look.

Spraying techniques

The mechanics of spraying water-based products are the same as those used to spray any other type of finish. The only differences are how you adjust the gun and how thick you apply the coating. Because water-based finishes are relatively thick, you may want to increase the size of the fluid tip on your gun. When spraying traditional lacquer, I usually use a tip in the .036-in. to .043-in. range. However, when working with water-based products, I increase the tip to .055 in. and in heavy production situations may use a tip that is as large as .086 in. The size tip you use depends on a combination of your equipment, spray technique, and personal preference. The main thing to consider is that the fluid tip on your gun should be big enough to apply a full wet coat but not so big that the gun doesn't atomize the fluid properly.

The relatively high solids content makes water-based finishes more prone to runs and sags than most other sprayed materials, so it is important to watch how heavy a coat you spray. The best way to apply a thick coat without creating any drips is to apply two light coats a few minutes apart. Spray the first coat just thick enough so that the surface is wet, wait a minute or two, then go back over the piece with a second light coat. The two thin coats will meld into one thick layer but will be much less likely to run or sag.

If you do get a drip or run, try to remove it immediately. A thick blob of water-based coating may take a long time to dry and when it finally does it will be difficult to sand. The best thing to do is to wipe off wet runs or drips with a clean, damp cloth and respray the area. In some cases, you may be able to delicately wipe the trouble spot without disturbing the surrounding area. However, more often than not you will

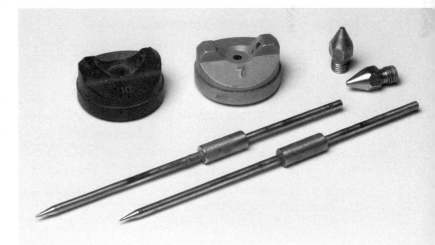

If you do a lot of spraying and use several different types of material, you will probably want to invest in more than one fluid tip/needle and air cap combination.

Water-based finishes have a tendency to build up on the fluid tip and air cap. When the deposits are wet, they are easy to remove with a fingernail or a toothpick. When they are dry, they must be cleaned off with warm water or even lacquer thinner.

in and out will result in a coat that is too thick in some places and too thin in others.

Because water-based products don't remelt themselves the way lacquer does, they have a tendency to build up around the fluid tip and horns on the air cap. If the buildup becomes too dense, the fluid flow or atomization air may become restricted to the point where the gun stops working properly. Fortunately, it is an easy problem to handle. First, you could switch to a larger fluid tip. Also, by holding the gun a few inches farther away from the surface, you can reduce the amount of bounceback that may be sticking to the tip.

If the finish does begin to build on the tip of the gun, simply remove it with your fingernail or a toothpick. Although the wet deposits are easy to scrape off, they dry and become hard fairly quickly. To make the finish easier to remove, try wiping a thin coat of spray-gun lubricant or Vaseline over the outside of the air cap and fluid tip before you begin spraying. Just be sure the lubricant you use is designed for spray equipment and contains no silicone, which can be found in regular household or machine oil. If silicone gets on your gun, it will be picked up by the finish and cause small crater-like depressions known as fisheye. Once silicone gets in a gun, it is hard to remove.

Finally, don't be concerned if a freshly sprayed coating has severe orange peel. This is a typical characteristic of water-based finishes. They go on rough but level out to a smooth surface. With some products, the orange peel will disappear almost immediately. Other finishes, along with overly thick coats, may take a bit longer to level out.

have to wipe the finish off the entire side or section. As long as your rag is clean and doesn't leave any lint on the surface, you shouldn't have too many problems. Simply wipe down the area in question until all of the wet finish is removed, then spray it again. If you don't see a drip until the next day, it is often easier to slice it off with a razor blade than it is to remove it with sandpaper.

As with all spraying, start in the least visible areas and work your way toward the sections that will be seen the most. Overlap each pass by about half, using a slow, steady motion. The objective is to lay down a full, wet coat that is even in thickness over the entire surface. Keep the gun the same distance from the surface at all times, being sure the tip is perpendicular to the area being sprayed. Tilting the gun at an angle or moving it

Guidelines for working with water-based finishes

- Do not use steel wool under or between water-based coatings.

- Remove sanding dust with damp rags, not tack cloths.

- Make sure the finishing room is warm and dry.

- Do not let products freeze.

- Use thinner sparingly or not at all.

- Make sure the finishing area has good air movement for safety and proper drying.

Brushing water-based finishes

- Use synthetic-bristle brushes.

- Keep finishes well-stirred but do not shake can.

- Do not scrape a wet brush on the side of the can.

- Flow finish on with long, smooth strokes but don't overbrush.

Spraying water-based finishes

- Strain finishes before spraying.

- Remove runs, drips, or sags immediately; they will be much harder to repair once dry.

- Wear a vapor respirator when spraying.

- Keep equipment clean and dry.

Sanding

One of the nice things about water-based finishes is they are fairly easy to sand. How much sanding you do depends on how well you prepare the surface and apply the finish. If you use spray equipment, you may not have to do much sanding at all. If you apply the finish with a brush, you may have a bit more work.

There are two reasons to sand water-based topcoats. The first, and most obvious, is to remove surface defects such as dust, bubbles, and brush marks. Generally the first coat will need the most sanding. Once it is dry, it should be given a thorough sanding with the appropriate grit paper. I usually sand the first coat with 240-grit wet/dry paper,

but what you use will depend on how rough the surface is. If there are a lot of large bubbles and deep brush marks, you may need to drop down to 180 grit. On the other hand, if you have done a good job sealing the wood and are careful how you apply the topcoat, you may be able to smooth the surface with a grit as high as 320. The goal of sanding the first coat of finish is to end up with a surface that is flat, smooth, and free of defects.

The second reason for sanding water-based products is that it helps create a better bond between coats of finish. Since water-based materials don't melt the previous coat of finish the way lacquers and shellac do, a second coat of finish may need a little help biting into the first. How much help is needed depends on how long the first coat has

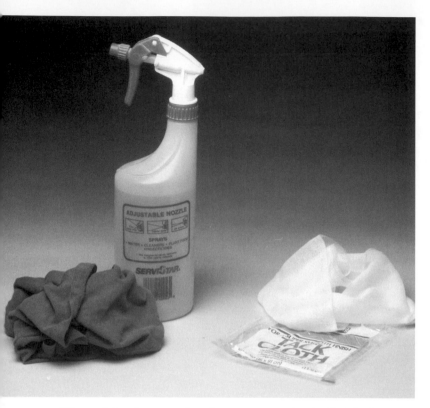

When wiping down sanding dust, use a rag that is slightly damp. Never use sticky tack cloths.

Finally, when you are done sanding, it is important to remove all of the dust. With lacquer or shellac this is not as important because the next coat of finish will redissolve the dust left from sanding the previous coat. However, water-based products are limited in their ability to redissolve, or melt, this dust. It must be removed before the next coat can be applied. The best way to clean the surface is to wipe it down with a damp rag. On large jobs, I like to thoroughly wet a clean rag, then ring it out as much as possible. On smaller jobs, I keep the rag moist by periodically misting it with a spray bottle. If the rag is too wet, it won't remove the dust but simply smear it all over the place. Keep the rag clean by rinsing it periodically.

Some people recommend wiping off the surface with mineral spirits but I avoid this. Mineral spirits may soften some water-based finishes, especially those that aren't fully cured. Water is the better choice because it is cheap, easy to use, won't harm the finish, and does a good job of removing the dust. Above all, don't use a tack cloth on a water-based finish. The resins used in tack cloths are sticky and don't react well with these finishes. I once used a tack cloth to wipe down a piece before applying the final coat. Everything went fine until a few days later when the customer called me back to look at the finish. Right there in the middle of a cabinet door were my fingerprints. The sticky residue on the tack cloth was transferred from my fingers to the wood and showed plain as day through the clear finish.

been allowed to dry. If you apply the coats relatively quickly, such as within a day of each other, they will bond together well with or without any sanding. However, if the first coat has been allowed to dry a few days or more, it will be hard and partially cured. The second coat will have more difficulty grabbing hold of the first coat. In this situation, it is a good idea to lightly etch the finish by taking very light passes with 320- or 400-grit paper. The resulting surface will feel hard and smooth but will contain enough small scratches for the next coat to bite into.

Pigmented Topcoats

Although it is nice to allow the natural beauty of wood to shine through, clear finishes are not appropriate for all pieces of furniture. At some point, you will want to give a piece an opaque, or painted, finish. This may be due to design considerations or may be necessary to cover up an inferior piece of wood. When working with opaque finishes, you have two choices: paint or pigmented lacquer. Although the final appearance may be similar, the materials are different and require different preparation and application techniques. Understanding these differences will not only help you choose which type of finish is right for your project but will also make working with them easier.

Latex paints

Latex paints were the first true water-based products to find their way to the consumer market. Like all finishes, latex paints consist of resins and pigments, which are suspended in various solvents and water. Latex paints have some definite advantages over other pigmented coatings. To begin with, they are readily available. You can walk into any paint or hardware store and find an entire section devoted to latex paints. Pigmented lacquers, on the other hand, are not commonly sold in hardware stores. To buy them, you may have to go to a well-equipped paint store or even a commercial distributor.

When compared with oil-based paints, cleaning up after using latex products is a breeze. Oil-based paints require the use of paint thinner or mineral spirits, which not only smells but must also be stored and disposed of properly. As with all water-based products, latex paints clean up with soap and water. Also, latex paints dry fast and are relatively easy to apply.

Of course, latex paints are not perfect. While they may be the ideal finish for surfaces that are not closely scrutinized, like walls, trim, or the side of a house, they are not always the best choice for fine furniture. Latex paints tend to be a bit duller in appearance than oil-based products. As a result, getting a hard, highly polished appearance with latex can be difficult and may require the application of a clear topcoat over the paint. In addition, latex paints are high in viscosity and can be tough to spray. If your spray system is undersized, you will have a hard time getting a smooth, furniture-quality finish with latex paint.

Water-based acrylic paints

When finishing fine furniture, a good alternative to latex paints are water-based acrylics. These finishes use newer resins and formulations than latex paints and are closer to lacquer than to paint in appearance and performance. Acrylics appear brighter and shinier than latex, they dry harder, and they are more durable. Water-based acrylics are a good choice when finishing colorful objects like children's furniture and toys.

Pigmented lacquers

Before using paint on your next project, you may want to consider pigmented lacquers as an alternative. Water-based pigmented lacquers are close relatives to latex paints. They consist of resins, pigments, and solvents mixed in water. The main difference lies in the types of resins and additives used to make the two products. In general, water-based pigmented lacquers are formulated with the newest technology and resins available. The resins are tougher yet more flexible. Lacquers atomize better than paint, flow out to a smoother coat, dry faster, and are easier to sand. In addition, they tend to be harder and will wear better than latex paint. Although it is usually a good idea to apply a clear topcoat as additional protection over any pigmented finish, it is not necessary with most of the lacquers on the market today. The products I use in my shop have all been approved for use on kitchen and bathroom cabinets and can withstand a lot of abuse.

Of course, pigmented lacquers do have a few drawbacks. They are designed to be used primarily by the furniture industry, so you may have to make a few phone calls before locating a distributor. You probably won't find these products in your average hardware store, but a well-stocked paint-supply store should have at least one brand on the shelf. You may find pigmented lacquers in one of the many woodworking mail-order catalogs as well. If you can't locate a supplier, try contacting the manu-facturers themselves. They will be more than happy to give you the name and number of the nearest dealer that carries their products.

Opaque pigmented lacquers make a good alternative to paint. They are easier to apply, dry faster, and look better on fine furniture.

Another potential stumbling block with pigmented lacquers is their cost. Although the price of most water-based products has come down over the past few years and continues to drop, they are still expensive when compared to paint. In fact, the water-based pigmented lacquer I use in my shop costs anywhere from 25% to 50% more than a gallon of latex paint. However, their ease of use and consistent results make them worth the extra cost.

Because most pigmented lacquers are used by professional wood finishers, they are designed to be used with spray equipment, not brushes. This does not mean that if you don't have a spray gun, these finishes are not an option. Many companies offer flow additives, extenders, or drying retarders that will make the lacquer easier to apply with a

brush. However, applying pigmented lacquers with a brush won't be easy and the results may be disappointing.

The final problem to consider when using pigmented lacquers is that you may have a hard time matching specific colors. Your local paint or hardware store will be happy to mix a custom color in cans as small as a quart. However, most distributors of pigmented lacquers deal in volume. They may be willing to mix a 5-gallon bucket for you, but chances are they won't deal with anything less than that. The alternative is to mix your own lacquer.

Matching paint colors is not an easy task. You need a good eye, the proper pigments, measuring devices and containers, plenty of extra lacquer, and a lot of patience. The very thought of trying to mix a batch of lacquer that

A few drops of premeasured pigments from your local paint store are all you need to match custom colors.

matches a specific paint sample may be overwhelming. However, I regularly mix my own colors with little or no fuss. I do this with the help of my local hardware store. When a customer asks me to match a certain color, I take a sample chip to the paint department. Their color-matching computer gives me a readout of the various pigments that make up that color. For a dollar or two the store will give me the correct amount of pigments in a paper cup, which I then mix into my own lacquer.

I should note that the final color may not be an exact match to the original sample. The resins used in water-based finishes often give them a slightly bluish tint, and this may be particularly noticeable with pigmented lacquers. As a result, since the water-based white you are using as a mixing base may be a slightly different (and bluish) shade from what was used as the base for your sample chip, the formula given to you by the computer may be a bit off. If you are looking for an exact match, you may have to tweak the formula a bit, but it should be fairly close. If nothing else, the formula gives you an idea of the various shades of pigments needed to form the color. I have been using this method of mixing pigmented lacquers for several years and have had only one customer complain that the color was not right.

Preparing the surface

As with any finish material, the keys to success lie in how the surface being finished is filled and sanded along with how the material is prepared and applied.

The first time I was hired to build a piece of painted furniture, I reasoned that since it would get an opaque finish I didn't have to worry too much about the quality of the wood, how well I sanded it, or how tight the joints were. After all, I reasoned, any defects could simply be filled and covered over with paint. I rushed through the production stages of the project, constantly telling myself not to worry about any major defects. "The paint will cover it" went through my mind several times throughout the course of putting the wall unit together.

When I began to apply the finish, I quickly realized I was in for a bit more than I had bargained for. In fact, a lot more. I sprayed a coat of latex primer over the cabinets, let it dry, then began to sand it smooth. I was concerned about the amount of defects that seemed to appear from nowhere, so I did what I thought was a thorough job of filling and caulking the major scratches, holes, cracks, and voids. The smaller holes and dings would be filled in with the paint, so I didn't worry about them.

I sanded the primer smooth and sprayed on the first of what I hoped would be two coats of paint. The paint went on well and seemed to be leveling out nicely, so I went home that night satisfied that I would be able to apply the second coat the next day and deliver the unit a day later as promised.

When I came in the next morning, I was surprised at the number of defects that still showed through the primer and first coat of paint. I wasn't worried though—some more filler and caulk and another coat of paint would do the trick. I repeated the filling and caulking process, sanded everything smooth, and sprayed what was to be the final coat.

Of course, I was nowhere near the final coat. The next day I was faced with the same problem as the day before. Voids, cracks, sanding scratches, and holes seemed to have appeared out of nowhere. Apparently I had not allowed enough time for the caulk and putty I applied the day before to dry. The putty showed signs of cracking, and the caulk appeared to be pulling away from the previous coat of paint. I was forced to repeat the entire process. This time I did a better job of sanding and filling and allowed much more time for everything to dry before applying the paint. Although the finish was greatly improved, I still had to run through the whole finishing sequence again before I got the results I wanted.

By the time I was done finishing the wall unit, I realized that the reason I got the job in the first place was probably because my bid was so low. I simply did not realize just how much work was involved in achieving a good painted finish.

This experience taught me a valuable lesson. Namely, that building and finishing a piece of furniture with an opaque finish requires the same care, skill, and effort that goes into a piece being finished with a clear topcoat. In fact, I feel that getting a high-quality finish on a piece of painted furniture is even harder and requires more work than when working with a clear finish. I often have customers ask me to quote a piece with the option of either a clear or a painted finish. When they hear the two prices, they almost always say they thought the painted finish would be substantially less. I explain while there may be savings by using a cheaper grade of wood (like substituting soft maple or poplar for cherry), the extra work that goes into the finish virtually negates any savings.

The clear finishes I have been talking about in this book will, to a certain extent, fill or hide small blemishes like scratches left by sanding. Opaque finishes, on the other hand, cause these blemishes to jump out. A tiny hole that may be nearly invisible under a stain or clear finish will be magnified by paint. This is especially true with high-gloss finishes, which bounce light back at you. Any defect in the wood causes the light to refract in different directions, drawing attention to the trouble spot. As a result, the quality of a painted finish depends on how well the piece is built, how well it is sanded, and how carefully it is filled, caulked and puttied, and primed.

CONSTRUCTION TECHNIQUES

When building painted furniture, you must use the same care in measuring, cutting, and joinery that you would when building a piece that will be clear finished. Although you can use a lesser grade of wood (I usually use either poplar or soft maple on painted projects), you should not skimp on sound construction techniques. Cleanly machined surfaces, tight-fitting joints, and thorough sanding are all necessary components of a smooth, blemish-free finish. While there will inevitably be the need for putty or caulk to fill cracks and voids, it would be a mistake to depend on them to correct poorly executed construction. The more patching compound you use, the more likely it is to crack or fall out at a later date. Likewise, joints that are gapped or loose will show through as cracks in the finish over time.

SANDING

Once your piece is fully machined and assembled, the last step before beginning the finishing process involves sanding all of the surfaces. The key here is not so much in how fine a grit you use but in how carefully you sand. In fact, using too fine a grit may cause more problems than it solves. Since pigmented finishes don't really penetrate the surface of the wood, they need a slight roughness to bite into. If you sand the wood too smooth with a high-grit paper, you may have adhesion problems. The freshly finished surface may look and feel great, but the paint or lacquer may chip or peel off with very little effort. For this reason, it is better to do a thorough job sanding the bare wood with a lower grit, then use progressively higher grits to smooth out the primer and topcoats. When working with pigmented topcoats, be it paint or lacquer, I generally sand to 120 or 150 grit before applying the first coat of primer.

Priming the surface

When I first began my own business, my partner and I did a lot of trim carpentry. We usually would apply a coat of primer to the trim before hanging it, especially on exterior work. In my mind the primer was there to protect the wood from the weather and seal in any defects like grease, crayon marks, and knots. How evenly or smoothly it was applied didn't really bother me, since the painters would be covering it over anyway. I have since learned that how well the primer coats are applied plays a great role in the appearance of the subsequent topcoat.

This is especially true when trying to achieve high-quality finishes on fine cabinets and furniture. In fact, I would say that applying and sanding the primer is the most important step in a pigmented topcoat finishing schedule.

Primers are, in basic terms, pigmented topcoats that have been reformulated to make them dry faster, seal in defects, adhere better, and easier to sand. Think of them as clear sealers that have pigments added to make them opaque.

WHY USE PRIMERS

It would be nice to be able to eliminate an entire process in any finishing schedule. The work would go faster and you wouldn't need to worry about introducing another type of material to the process. In fact, if you wanted to finish a piece by simply applying the paint or lacquer directly to the bare wood you could. But I doubt you would like the results. To begin with, the finish probably wouldn't stick to the surface very well. It would appear bumpy, and knots, sap pockets, and grease on the wood would eventually bleed through. Worst of all, it would be difficult to sand the finish without leaving ugly scratches or even removing the coating entirely.

Primers prevent all of this from happening by performing three key roles. First, they act as sealers, locking in surface imperfections such as variations in color, wax, grease, sap, and knots that would otherwise bleed through the finish. Second, their bulk allows them to act as pore fillers, helping to create a smooth, even surface. Third, primers contain a high ratio of binders to pigment along with various acids that help them bite into a surface better than

If you try to cover a defect like this knot without using a primer first, it will eventually bleed through the finish, no matter how many coats of paint or lacquer you apply.

a topcoat can. They also contain products known as flatting agents that reduce the gloss or shine of the primer. The subsequent topcoat will adhere much better to a dull surface than to a shiny one. As a result, primers act as effective adhesion agents, strengthening the bond between the wood and the topcoat.

Not only are primers important from a technical viewpoint but they are also practical. Primers are designed to dry fast, which means you can apply the topcoat a few hours later. They are also easy to sand, allowing you to obtain a smooth, flat surface with relatively little effort. In addition, primers are less expensive than pigmented topcoats, which makes them very cost effective.

PREPARING PRIMERS

Depending on the type of primer and your method of application, the primer may need no preparation prior to use. If you are applying a latex primer with a brush, simply open the can, stir it thoroughly, and you're ready to start painting. If you are using a pigmented lacquer primer and a spray gun, you have a bit more work to do.

Pigmented lacquer primers are extremely thick liquids that usually contain a high percentage of solids. Most two- and three-stage turbines do not generate enough air pressure to adequately atomize these materials. You may be able to spray them with some success, but chances are the primer will come out in relatively large clumps that won't flow together properly. The resulting film will be bumpy and hard to sand. The same may be true even if you are using a good-quality compressed-air system with a large compressor.

In all likelihood, you will have to thin primers first if you are going to spray them. Some manufacturers provide flow additives designed specifically for thinning their products. These additives contain a mixture of water and slow-drying alcohols that is compatible with the composition of their primers. In reality, these additives are nothing more than expensive water. If you have to thin a primer and don't have or don't want to pay for a flow additive, simply use tap water. Cold water may make the finish sluggish or lumpy, so if possible use water that is at least room temperature. Warm water is even better—it will make the primer handle better and flow out more evenly.

Be careful not to overthin the primer. You want to get it thin enough to spray but not so thin that it runs off the surface. Too much thinner may also weaken the resulting film or lessen the primer's ability to hide defects. Chances are the label on the can will tell you how

If your spray gun is underpowered, it won't atomize thick liquids like pigmented primers properly. The resulting finish will be lumpy and rough.

much the product can be thinned. If the instructions don't indicate how much thinner to use, add a little at a time until the material is just thin enough to fully atomize.

Be sure to stir pigmented primers thoroughly before filling the cup or pressure pot. The various solids in primers have a tendency to settle out of suspension relatively quickly, forming a thick, gooey sludge on the bottom of the can. If you don't stir the primer, you may end up with a spray gun full of what amounts to colored water.

Like all water-based finishes, the primer should be run through a strainer before you begin spraying. Primer dries fast and tends to form on the rim and sides of the can fairly quickly. When you open the can and stir it up, these dried particles will fall into the finish and eventually find their way into your gun. All it takes is one tiny clump of dried finish or congealed solids to plug up your gun. Because primers are thick, they may take awhile to flow through a strainer, but it is well worth the effort if it saves you from having to drain your gun and clean it out in the middle of a project.

APPLYING PRIMERS

In general, primers are applied just as any other water-based topcoat. The idea is to lay down a full, wet coat that is as smooth and even as possible. The beauty of working with primers is that if you make a mistake it is easy to fix.

Brushing The type of brush used when working with water-based primers should be the same as when working with topcoats. The basic technique used for brushing primers is the same as well.

Wet the brush with water first, then dip it one-third to one-half the way into the primer before flowing on a smooth, even coat.

The are two main differences between brushing primers and topcoats. The first concerns the speed with which the primer dries while the second relates to how the primer is absorbed into the wood. Primer dries fast, and even if you work quickly it may not always be possible to work from a wet edge. Don't worry about slight lap marks—they will be easy to remove by sanding. Severe brush or lap marks will require much more effort to sand, so try to keep the coat as smooth as possible. Primers will also be absorbed into the pores of the wood much more than a topcoat, especially on roughly sanded surfaces and end grain. As a result, you must apply an even coat over the entire

Compared with side grain, end grain soaks up so much primer that it may look as though none was applied.

surface. The chances of sanding through the primer to bare wood are greatly increased if the coat is thick in some places but too thin in others.

Spraying Other than the potential need for a significant amount of thinner, primers are sprayed just as any other topcoat. The gun should be adjusted so the material is properly atomized and flows out in a smooth, wet coat. While you don't want to put the primer on so thick that it runs, you may want to spray a slightly heavier layer than you would with a pigmented topcoat. In fact, because the primer I use dries so fast, I often spray a piece and immediately go back over the entire thing in the opposite direction. This assures that I have a full, even coat with no thin spots, skips, or misses.

Dry primer is a joy to sand. The sandpaper glides over the surface easily, creating a fine powder while leaving behind a shiny, smooth surface.

SANDING AND RECOATING

Once the primer is dry, you can begin the sanding and filling process. Under ideal conditions, most primers dry fast and should be ready to sand in no more than an hour. The primer I use is often ready to sand in 15 to 20 minutes, but when it is cold or especially humid I may have to wait an hour or two. If the sandpaper glides effortlessly over the primer, causing it to form a light, fluffy powder while leaving behind a smooth, satiny surface, the primer is dry enough to sand. If the paper drags across the surface and clogs up with a gummy residue while leaving behind clumps and streaks on the surface, the primer needs to dry a bit longer.

I usually sand the first coat of primer with a 220- or 240-grit wet/dry paper. I do not use water when sanding for a few reasons. The primer probably contains some type of lubricant and it should sand quite easily on its own. I also don't like to use water because of the mess it makes. Finally, I usually use an electric palm sander for at least some of this initial sanding, so it makes sense to avoid water.

You should sand the first coat of primer thoroughly, being sure to smooth out any raised grain, rough spots, brush marks, blemishes, and areas where the primer was applied unevenly. Sanding this first coat of primer may create a feeling of mixed emotions. On the one hand, dry primer is fun to sand. It takes very little effort to create a smooth, soft surface that gives you your first glimpse of how the finished piece will look. On the other hand, every tiny imperfection will suddenly become extremely visible. Marks, dings, gapped joints, and scratches will seem to appear out of nowhere. This is where the real work begins. Each and every one of these surface imperfections must be patched, filled, or repaired or else they will become more noticeable with each coat of finish that is applied. The key here is to go over the entire piece carefully, being sure to fill, caulk, spackle, or otherwise repair every defect. Use a strong light held at several different angles and take your time. The more thorough you are here the less work you will have to do later.

While you could fill all of the defects before applying the first coat of primer, I like to wait for two reasons. First, the primer makes the defects easier to see. Second, it helps the patch adhere to the surface much better.

I use a fast-drying water-based wood putty for small repairs and may resort to caulk, wall spackle, or even epoxy for major cracks and problem areas. Be sure to allow whatever filler material you use to dry thoroughly before sanding and recoating. If the patch is still wet when you apply the second coat, it may shrink or crack and show through the final finish days or weeks later.

Once all of your repair work is dry, go back over everything with an appropriate grit sandpaper. If you are extremely good, or lucky, you may have a few very small spots that can be sanded smooth with the same paper you used on the primer. If not, you may have to drop down to a lower grit. If you do use a lower grit paper, it is not necessary to resand it with the higher grit. The next coat of primer will fill the scratches and then you can sand the entire piece smooth.

Once sanded, the piece is ready for a second coat of primer. Apply the second coat just as the first, paying special attention to the areas that were filled or patched. If the patches were relatively large, you may want to spot-prime them first, then go over them again as you coat the entire piece.

After allowing the second coat of primer to dry, sand it with the next highest grit paper. This sanding should be lighter and less aggressive than the first. At this point, you are trying to create a surface that is perfectly smooth and free of voids. If all has gone well, you should be able to sand the entire piece lightly in preparation for applying the topcoat. However, things don't always go according to plan, and you may be faced with another round of patching and filling followed by another coat of primer.

It is always tempting to rush through the priming stage and get right to the color coat. Although you could use the finish coats to get a smooth, even surface, it is far better to take care of any problems while still at the priming stage. The primer is easier to apply, sands easier, fills gaps and covers problems better, and costs less. In general, you will get a better finish with three coats of primer and one topcoat than you will with one coat of primer followed by three topcoats.

Applying the topcoat

Once the piece has been properly primed and sanded, you are ready to apply the final color coat, often called the "money coat." Again, whether you are using paint or pigmented lacquer, the basic application equipment and techniques are, with a few exceptions, the same.

BRUSHING PAINT

Latex and acrylic paints usually need little or no preparation before applying with a brush. The paint should simply be well stirred and poured into a separate clean container.

Painting a piece of furniture or a cabinet uses the same techniques outlined on pp. 99-103. Remember that the object is to flow the material onto the surface as smoothly and evenly as possible. Because this is the last coat of finish, you want to avoid brush and lap marks as much as you can. Just as when applying clear coats, work from the least visible areas first. Always start a brushstroke a few inches in from an edge or corner and then go back in the other direction to complete the surface. Because most paints dry a bit slower than clear topcoats, you don't have to work quite as fast, and you'll have more time to go back over a wet surface with light brushstrokes to remove any bumps, ridges, or lap marks. Most paints do a good job of leveling out after they have been applied, so there is no need to overwork the finish with the brush.

SPRAYING PAINT

If you decide to spray latex or acrylic paint, there are a few things to consider. First, paints are relatively heavy-bodied materials and, depending on your spray equipment, may need to be thinned a bit. If your equipment is undersized, the paint won't atomize properly, and you may end up with a coat that is rough and mottled or may contain a severe case of orange peel. Water will work as a thinner, but as with all high-solids products be careful how much you add. A better alternative is to use one of the flow-additive products designed specifically for spraying latex paint. These additives are not thinners, but they will make the paint seem a bit lighter and easier to spray. Their real purpose is to help the paint flow out better into a smoother, more even coat. Be warned that one of the ways additives do this is by slowing down the drying time of the paint, which means there is greater chance for dust to settle in the finish.

SPRAYING PIGMENTED LACQUERS

Pigmented lacquers are simple to prepare for spraying. Like all water-based finishes, they must be thoroughly stirred and poured through a strainer. Because pigmented topcoats are not as thick as primers, they can usually be sprayed without any thinner. However, if you do need to add thinner, remember that these products are a delicate mixture of chemicals and have a relatively high solids content. If you add too much thinner, whether it is water or a manufacturer-recommended flow additive, you could upset the balance of the mixture and end up with a material that runs all over and won't dry properly.

The mechanics of spraying pigmented lacquers is no different from those used when spraying pigmented primers. Your goal should be to lay down a full, wet coat that contains no skips or misses. Ideally, the primed and sanded surface should be so smooth and close to perfect that you need only one topcoat to achieve a uniform finish. If you create a

Too much thinner may cause heavy-bodied pigmented lacquers to run and sag. If you do get drips, remove them while they are still wet.

problem spot when spraying, like a run, drip, or large thumbprint, it is easier to correct it immediately than it is to repair it when it is dry.

Unlike primers, which are easy to sand, topcoats don't sand as well. If you need to apply a second topcoat, you should do it soon after the first coat has dried. If you apply the second coat within a few hours after the first, you won't need to sand to avoid adhesion problems. However, if you wait more than a day, you should scuff the first coat with sandpaper to give the second coat something to bite into. If this is the case or if you simply think the topcoat is too rough and needs to be sanded, work carefully with a fine grit paper. In these situations, I use a 400- or 600-grit paper and take light passes in the direction of the grain. The topcoat will not powder up as much as the primer and will be more difficult to sand. Avoid the

temptation to really attack the finish since large scratches left in the surface of a pigmented lacquer topcoat are hard to remove and may show through the second coat.

PROTECTING THE FINISH

It may seem silly to talk about protecting the material that was applied as protection in the first place, but in some cases you may want to apply a clear finish over a pigmented topcoat. Clear topcoats may also be used to add a greater sense of depth to the finish or to change the shine. Latex paint in particular tends to appear flat or dull, so a clear coat of gloss lacquer may be used to increase the shine. In fact, with most paints and some lacquers you will work less and get better results by coating a satin or flat finish with clear gloss than you would by applying a pigmented gloss topcoat.

9

Final Steps

If you apply your topcoats with a good-quality spray gun over a properly prepared surface under ideal conditions, you may get lucky and end up with a perfect finish that needs no additional work. However, more likely than not, the final coat of finish will contain some unevenness or imperfections that need to be removed. This is especially true if you apply your finishes with a brush. No matter how careful you are and how good your technique is, chances are the final coat will contain small specks of dust, bubbles, and brush marks. In some cases, these defects will be small and unnoticeable. If the defects are on drawer parts or cabinet backs and won't be seen, no further steps are necessary. But if you are working on a visible area and want a smooth, high-quality finish, such as on a tabletop, you will have to rub out the final coat.

If you were to ask five woodworkers the steps they take when rubbing out a finish, I bet you would get five different responses. But even though everyone may have his own specific materials and methods, the basic principles are the same. The materials you use, including finish, types and grits of sandpaper, and rubbing compounds, may be a matter of personal preference, but if you follow the guidelines listed here you should get good results on a consistent basis.

Why rub out a finish?

When you rub out a finish, you are doing three things: removing surface imperfections like dust, leveling the finish so it is perfectly flat, and creating a fine scratch pattern that produces the desired sheen. Technically, a finish does

There are numerous materials that can be used to rub out a finish. Which you choose is largely a matter of personal preference.

not need to be rubbed out since the process does nothing to improve the finish's ability to protect the underlying wood. However, rubbing out is often the difference between a "nicc" finish and a "great" one. Rubbing out thc final coat not only allows you to adjust the sheen but also gives the piece an appearance of warmth and smoothness that is visible to the eye and can be felt as well. A finish that has been rubbed out to a smooth, consistent shine will have a silky, tactile quality associated with the finest pieces of furniture.

The basic process for rubbing out a water-based finish is no different than that for a solvent-based lacquer or varnish. First, you remove surface imperfections by sanding with fine-grit papers. Next, you flatten the surface, removing high and low spots in the finish. Finally, you use a rubbing compound to produce an even, consistent scratch pattern over the entire piece. There are, however, some differences that must be taken into account when using water-based finishes. How the surface is prepared, the type of finish used, and how it is applied are all critical to success when rubbing out water-based finishes.

Preparing the surface

A good finish begins with good surface preparation. This is especially true when working with open-grained woods like oak and mahogany. If you wish to achieve a smooth, high-quality finish that has a nice look and feel, it is important to begin by using a pore filler to fill the grain of the wood. If you do not fill the pores, obtaining the soft, silky feel of a flat, well-rubbed finish will be difficult. You could use the finish to fill open pores by building layer upon layer, but this will require more coats and a lot more work than necessary.

Selecting a finish

Just like traditional lacquers and varnishes, not all water-based products rub out the same. Some are fairly easy to work with and can be rubbed out to a high gloss, while others can be temperamental and no matter how much you rub will always appear dull. When choosing a water-based finish that you know will be rubbed out, look for one that has acrylic resin in the formula. (The major ingredients, including resins and solvents, should be listed on the can.) Acrylic resins are relatively hard and brittle and are easy to scratch. This makes them much easier to rub out than urethanes. Urethanes, which are extremely tough and flexible, don't scratch very well. As a result, they can be difficult to rub to a high gloss.

If you are unsure about the rubbing characteristics of a particular product, you could contact the manufacturer, but I suspect they will all claim their products are unsurpassed in their ability to be rubbed to a high shine. Other woodworkers may be able to share their experiences with a certain brand, but when in doubt, a test panel is still the best way to determine if you like the way a finish feels and handles. Once you find something you like, stick with it and you should get good results every time.

The other factor to consider when selecting a topcoat is whether you want a flat, satin, or high-gloss finish. While the rubbing-out process is used to create the desired level of shine, selecting the right material is the first and most important step. Finishes labeled as gloss are the most versatile, since they can be rubbed to a high-gloss shine or can be dulled, or rubbed down, to a semigloss or satin.

If you use a satin or matte finish, you will be more limited in how much control you have over the final appearance of the film. Matte, satin, and semigloss products are basically gloss finishes that have flatting agents added to the mix. Flatting agents are finely ground powders, or pigments, that deflect light, thus creating a duller, flatter appearance. While you may be able to take a satin finish and rub it up to a slightly higher gloss, this is a difficult process and requires a lot of work. An easier method is to start with a gloss finish and buff it down to the desired sheen.

In my shop I almost always use gloss products so that I am not limited in how

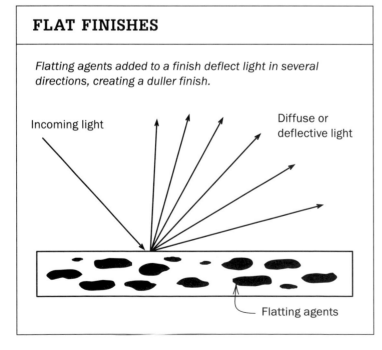

FLAT FINISHES

Flatting agents added to a finish deflect light in several directions, creating a duller finish.

Incoming light

Diffuse or deflective light

Flatting agents

the final finish appears. I learned this the hard way when a customer requested a satin finish on a table I made for him. I used a satin topcoat and lightly buffed the finish. When I delivered the table, the owner complained that it was not shiny enough. I patiently explained that the sample finish he chose was satin, which is what I gave him. Yes, he replied, but it's not shiny enough. If I had started with a gloss topcoat, I could have simply brought the piece back to the shop, rubbed it up to a gloss, and brought it back the same day. Instead, I had to apply a coat of gloss finish, let it dry for several days, then rub it out to a high shine. When I finally delivered the table a week later, the owner exclaimed, "That's the shiny satin finish I wanted!"

Applying the final coat

Water-based finishes don't always do a good job of "melting in" from one coat to the next the way shellac and lacquer do. In fact, some water-based finishes don't melt in at all—they form separate and distinct layers. Rubbing out these types of finishes becomes a bit tricky. If you remove too much of the top layer of finish, you will expose the previous coat. The area that is worn through will be clearly visible as lines or shadows. This can be a real problem if you are using tinted layers of finish to build color. Once they occur, these witness lines are difficult to repair. Depending on the type of finish you are using and how much skill (and luck) you have, you may be able to apply another coat of finish over the trouble spot and feather it lightly into the surrounding area. Once the finish is dry, you can sand the patched area in the hopes of blending it

in with the rest of the finish. In most cases, however, the only way to remove witness lines is to recoat the entire piece and start the rubbing process from the beginning.

Obviously, you must be very careful when rubbing out any finish. This is especially true near edges and sharp corners, where the finish may be thin to begin with and the tendency is to cut through by oversanding or rubbing too much. The best way to avoid witness lines is to make sure the final coat is a bit thicker than normal. You can do this one of two ways. The first, and most obvious, is to apply one thick final coat. If brushing, flow on more material than usual and don't spread it around as much. If using spray equipment, increase the fluid pressure, use a larger fluid tip, or simply move the gun closer to the surface and make slower passes. Making the final coat thicker should give you enough of a protective buffer zone of finish that rubbing through to the underlying layer is unlikely.

While this approach will help reduce the chances of rubbing through the finish, it does present a few problems. First, the high solids content of water-based finishes means they are best applied in thin rather than thick coats. If you put the finish on too thick, it may run or sag, especially on vertical surfaces. Second, a thick coat takes longer to dry, which means dust and other contaminants have more time to settle into the finish. If the finish is too thick, it may not dry properly at all, pulling away from sharp corners or developing a textured, mottled appearance.

A better way to apply the final coat is to do it in multiple stages separated by some drying time. If you are brushing

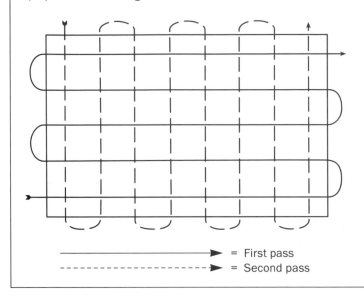

SPRAYING AN EVEN COAT

To apply a heavy, even coat with a spray gun, work in a box pattern, making the first pass with the grain and the second perpendicular to the grain.

```
————————————————▶ = First pass
- - - - - - - - - - -▶ = Second pass
```

overboard with this procedure, since placing too many wet coats on top of one another may cause the finish to wrinkle or not dry properly.

The same principles hold true when applying finish with a spray gun. For example, when finishing a large, flat surface like a tabletop, begin the final coat by misting on a very light yet fully wet film in the direction of the grain. As soon as the top is coated, repeat the process perpendicular to the grain (this spray pattern is known as boxing). Sprayed finishes dry much faster than those applied with a brush, so you should have no problem making the second set of passes immediately after the first. After letting the finish dry for no more than 10 minutes, repeat the process. When dry, the final coat will be at least twice as thick as normal, which will greatly reduce the chance of cutting through and creating shadows and witness lines.

Finally, most water-based finishes take a long time to fully cure when compared with nitrocellulose lacquer and shellac. The longer you wait before rubbing out the finish, the better. You should let the finish dry for at least a week, but waiting a month would be even better. A finish that has not fully cured can be rubbed to a flat or satin shine, but getting a high-gloss sheen will be impossible. You'll know the finish needs more curing time if no matter how much and how hard you rub, it won't go beyond a satiny shine. This can be a problem for professional woodworkers who need to move things out the door as soon as possible, but the final results justify the wait.

the finish, apply a very light, thin coat, let it sit until it is dry to the touch, then put on another light coat. Depending on the weather conditions and the material you are using, you may be able to apply the next coat in a few minutes or you may have to wait a bit longer. The finish should be dry enough so that the second application does not disturb or pull up the previous coat but not so dry that the finish is already hard. Since the first application is still soft, the second will bond with it much better, forming a thicker, more continuous film that will be harder to rub through. A third application in this manner should give you a final film that is thick enough for sanding and rubbing out without fear of witness lines. Be careful you don't go

Rubbing compounds

It seems that every woodworker I know swears that the compounds he uses to rub out finishes are the best. Some like theirs premixed, while others use powders. Some use wax as a lubricant, while others use mineral oil or water. While one may purchase his rubbing compounds from a woodworking supply house, others say that auto supply stores are the place to go. What you use really depends on two things: availability and personal preference. Given the choice, I prefer premixed pastes. I find them to be easier to use and I get better results. The problem with paste compounds is that some of them may contain solvents such as mineral spirits that react with dried water-based finish, softening the surface. While this won't affect the overall protective capabilities of the film, it will cause the finish to appear cloudy or hazy. For this reason, I avoid premixed pastes when working with water-based topcoats and use pumice and rottenstone.

Pumice, which is a ground-up lightweight volcanic rock, and rotten-stone, which is finely ground limestone, come in powder form. Pumice is graded just as steel wool, from F to 4F according to its coarseness. While you can premix these powders in a separate container with water or mineral oil, it is easier to mix them right on the surface being rubbed by pouring some out and then working them around with a soft cloth that has been soaked in the lubricant. Some people claim that using mineral oil will bring up a higher shine, but I generally use clean water as the lubricant.

When rubbing out water-based finishes, it is better to use rottenstone and pumice rather than premixed pastes, which may contain solvents that could soften the finish.

Rubbing out the finish

The techniques used to rub out a finish vary from one woodworker to the next, but the basic principles are the same. Following are the techniques I use to obtain flat, satin, and gloss finishes.

RUBBING TO A FLAT OR SATIN FINISH

Rubbing a finish to a flat or satin sheen is a relatively easy process and not nearly as labor intensive as rubbing out a gloss finish. Begin by removing any surface imperfections with 400-grit wet/dry sandpaper. If you have done a good job applying the final coat, this sanding can

How rubbing out works

Probably the best way to explain how the rubbing-out process changes the sheen of a topcoat is to compare the finishes to common treatments of aluminum. A polished piece of aluminum is very smooth and contains almost no scratches. As a result, a very high percentage of the light hitting the surface of the aluminum is reflected straight back up, making it appear shiny, almost mirrorlike. Brushed aluminum, on the other hand, has been etched with a rough wheel or brush and contains visible scratches. These scratches bounce or deflect the light in several directions, which means the light that comes back to your eye has been scattered, or diffused, and is not as intense. Therefore, a surface with scratches on it appears duller than one that is smooth or

The polished aluminum on the right reflects a high percentage of light, while the brushed sample on the left deflects light in several directions, creating a duller, or satin, shine.

be done very lightly with only your hand backing up the sandpaper. If the final coat contains a lot of imperfections or appears rough and uneven, you may have to drop to a 320-grit paper and use a wood or cork block to provide even pressure over the entire surface.

Once the defects have been removed and the finish is flat and level, begin rubbing it with 0000 steel wool or the equivalent-grade synthetic pad. Move the steel wool in long strokes, parallel with the grain, until the entire surface looks dull or flat. The goal is to create a scratch pattern that is straight and consistent, so try not to swing your hand in an arc or make swirling motions as you change direction at the end of each polished. The more and deeper the scratches, the more the light is scattered and the duller the surface appears.

When you rub out a finish, you put a series of scratches in the surface of the film that determines how much light is reflected and how shiny the surface is. If you put in a lot of deep, unevenly spaced scratches, you will have a dull or flat finish. Using successively finer grits of sandpaper and rubbing compounds allows you to create a fine pattern of shallow scratches, and thus a shine. Sanding a surface perfectly flat with a fine grit paper and then rubbing it with extremely fine compounds puts so many tiny scratches in the surface that it becomes, for all practical purposes, smooth. While a small amount of light is still deflected from the finish, so much of it is reflected back up that the surface looks like a mirror.

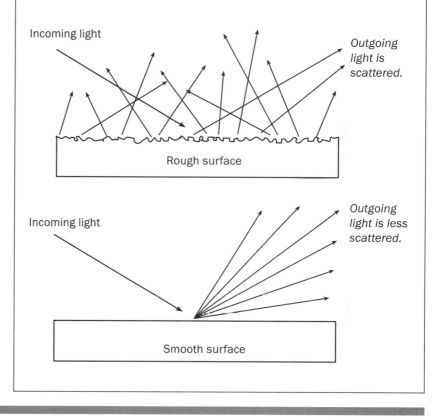

SURFACE SCRATCHES AND SHEEN

Deep, irregular scratches in a finish scatter light in several directions, making the light reflected back to your eye appear more diffuse or duller. A flat, smooth surface that contains very fine scratches reflects more light, making it appear brighter or shinier.

Incoming light

Outgoing light is scattered.

Rough surface

Incoming light

Outgoing light is less scattered.

Smooth surface

stroke. Be sure to remove any shiny spots, and pay particular attention to edges and corners where the tendency to cut through the finish is greatest.

If you want a flat, or matte, finish, you are done. However, rubbing to a satin finish requires an additional step. Once again, rub the surface with a clean piece of 0000 steel wool or a synthetic pad,

working in long, even strokes that overlap each other and are parallel with the grain. But this time, use a lubricant to bring up the sheen from flat to satin. The lubricant can be a premade mixture designed specifically for rubbing with steel wool or you can use wax. You can also use mineral oil or plain soapy water as a lubricant. Whatever you use, the

Begin the rubbing-out process by using wet/dry sandpaper to remove surface imperfections.

Use very fine 0000 steel wool to dull the entire surface, giving it a flat, or matte, finish.

main thing is that the lubricant must be nonabrasive so it won't interfere with the creation of an even, consistent scratch pattern.

Rub the entire surface evenly, checking your progress frequently. It should not take long before the finish begins to exhibit a soft, lustrous glow. Once you are done, use a clean, soft cloth or paper towels to remove the lubricant from the surface. If you used wax as a lubricant, you may have to buff it off with a clean piece of steel wool. Wet the steel wool with water and press very lightly on the surface to remove any residue. Any lubricant left behind will dry on the surface of the finish, creating smudges or dull spots.

While a satin finish may not be appropriate for a high-end piece of furniture like a dining table, the warm glow and soft feel of this type of finish looks good on just about anything. Satin finishes are not only easy to achieve but because they deflect light in several directions are also very forgiving. Surface imperfections that would stand out in a highly polished gloss finish may be invisible when the finish is rubbed to a satin sheen. This makes satin finishes ideal for open-grained woods like oak and mahogany, especially if a pore filler has not been used.

RUBBING TO A GLOSS FINISH

The initial steps taken when rubbing to a gloss finish are the same as when rubbing to a satin shine. First, you want to remove any surface imperfections by sanding with an appropriate wet/dry paper. The grit you choose when creating a gloss finish depends on how

A final rubbing with a lubricant and new 0000 steel wool or a synthetic pad like the one shown here gives the surface the warm glow and silky feel of a satin finish.

rough the final coat of finish is. To achieve a truly high-gloss shine, the finish must be perfectly flat and level, with no high or low spots. Therefore, if the last coat went on well, you may be able to start with a 400-grit paper. If, on the other hand, the finish is rough or uneven, it will be quicker and easier to drop to a lower grit. Usually 320 grit should work, but I have on at least one occasion started the rubbing process by sanding with a 240-grit paper. (Yes, I did a lousy job applying the final coat.) If you do need to use a lower grit, be careful of how much finish you remove, especially on the edges and corners of the piece.

When sanding prior to rubbing out a gloss finish, I always use a wood or cork backer block to ensure the finish is being leveled evenly. For the initial flattening

Rubbing compounds or lubricants left on the surface will dry to a dull haze, so it is important to thoroughly clean the surface with a damp cloth.

What is sheen?

I'm sure most people recognize the difference between a satin and gloss finish quite easily. After all, the names are fairly descriptive of how the finishes look. But I suspect fewer people are aware that finish manufacturers use a machine, called a gloss meter, to measure, or quantify, the amount of sheen contained in a finish.

A gloss meter measures sheen by bouncing light off the finish at a specific angle and measuring how much of that light is reflected back up at the same angle. Finish manufacturers generally use 60° as a standard and refer to the percentage of light reflected at that angle. Thus, a can of finish or product data sheet may read, "Sheen (60° meter): Gloss 85."

While the exact percentage of light reflected by a product labeled gloss by one manu-facturer may vary from that of another, all manufacturers use general guidelines when labeling

their products. Gloss finishes reflect 80% or more of the light; semigloss coatings range from 60% to 80%; and satin finishes can be anywhere from 30% to 60%. Anything that reflects less than 30% of the light at a 60° angle may be referred to as flat, eggshell, matte, or dull.

A gloss meter and its findings are important for keeping manufacturers consistent and

honest in how they label their products. I have even had commercial customers specify a certain degree of sheen for their projects. But the best way to determine the sheen of a finish is to look at it. If it is shiny, reflects a lot of light, and throws back a clear, sharp image of an object placed on it, it is gloss. If it is dull and reflects little or no light, it is flat. If it has a soft, warm glow that falls somewhere between flat and gloss, it is satin or semigloss.

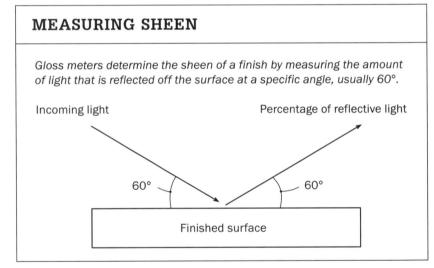

MEASURING SHEEN

Gloss meters determine the sheen of a finish by measuring the amount of light that is reflected off the surface at a specific angle, usually 60°.

Incoming light

Percentage of reflective light

60°   60°

Finished surface

stage, I sand at a 45° angle to the grain, working in two directions, then finish by sanding with the grain. Sanding at angles to the direction of the grain ensures the surface is even and flat with no valleys or low spots, which would show up as shiny areas.

Once the surface is smooth, dull, and level, switch to the next highest grit and repeat the sanding process. Again, use a backer block to keep the paper flat on the surface, but this time move with the direction of the grain. Continue until the scratches left by the previous grit have been removed. With each subsequent grit, the surface should appear slightly brighter or shinier. For most pieces I finish, I stop sanding with 600-grit paper, but you can go as high as you like. Obviously, the finer the grit you use, the less rubbing you will have to do to achieve a nice shine. However, you still have a long way to go.

Next, you are ready to start rubbing. As mentioned, on solvent-based finishes I like to use premixed rubbing pastes, but on water-based finishes I use pumice and rottenstone. I begin by applying a liberal amount of 4F pumice to the surface, then rub it with a clean, damp cotton cloth. The objective is to create a series of fine scratches that are so small they are practically invisible, so it doesn't matter what direction you move the cloth. I generally work in circular motions simply because it is easiest. The most important thing is to apply very firm pressure while rubbing the entire surface. If you don't begin to feel tired or break a sweat, you're not rubbing hard enough.

With coarse compounds it is still quite easy to cut through the surface, so check your progress frequently by wiping off small areas with a clean cloth. As you rub, the compound will become dry and lumpy. Sprinkling some lubricant on the surface or dampening the cloth as needed will help the rubbing go easier.

Continue to rub until the entire surface appears uniform. At this point, the finish will be shinier than satin but will still appear somewhat dull or hazy. You will probably even be able to see the fine scratches left by the rubbing compound, but they will be removed in the next and final step.

To bring your finish to a glossy shine, wipe the surface with a clean, damp

Working in circular motions ensures the scratch pattern is even over the entire piece and is less tiring than working strictly back and forth.

cloth to remove all of the pumice, which might otherwise continue to scratch the surface. Next, rub the surface with rottenstone, applying it with firm, even pressure and working in any direction you want. As you check your progress, you will see a shine developing that gets brighter and clearer the more you rub. Although the chances of cutting through the finish with this final rubbing are greatly reduced, they still exist, so work carefully and pay attention to potential trouble spots.

Someone once asked me how I know when I'm done rubbing out a finish. That's a good question. Unfortunately, I don't have a good answer other than to say, "I just know." When you reach the point of diminishing returns, where more rubbing doesn't seem to increase the shine, it's time to stop. (Another way to tell it's time to stop is when your arms feel like they are made of lead.) There is

A final rubbing with rottenstone brings the surface to a high shine.

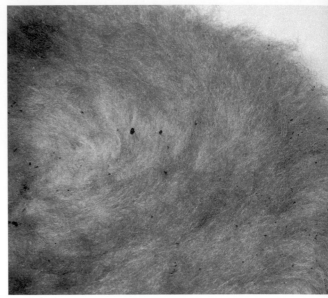

Power buffers make for fast work, but a clump of dried rubbing compound stuck in the pad can scratch the surface.

no doubt that rubbing out a finish is hard work, but standing back and looking at a highly polished surface is probably one of the most rewarding moments for any woodworker.

Using power buffers

When I have a number of pieces to rub out or an especially large table, I sometimes resort to using a soft lamb's-wool pad on the end of a grinder or drill to aid in the process. Although a power buffer will take some of the strain off your arms and make the work go faster, there are a couple of things to watch out for when using them to rub out a finish.

First, the friction created by a fast-moving buffer can generate a lot of heat, which in turn may soften the finish. The longer the finish has had to cure the less

likely this is to happen. But a relatively new finish may soften and become streaky or gummy. Also, the fluffy, soft pads on buffers have a tendency to hide small clumps of dried rubbing compound. When you switch from a coarse to a fine compound, any residue stuck to the pad will leave rather large and noticeable scratches that can only be removed by going back to that compound and starting the process over again. If you do plan to use a power buffer, be sure to keep the pad clean at all times or switch to a new pad with each change of grit.

Maintaining the finish

One of the nice things about the newest generation of water-based finishes is that they dry hard and can withstand a fair amount of abuse. Unlike oil and wax finishes, which need replenishing from time to time, water-based finishes ideally should need no maintenance other than an occasional cleaning with a soft cloth. Using common sense, such as keeping a dark piece out of bright sunlight and using coasters and hot plates on tables, will help protect a finish, allowing it to look as good years after the day it was first applied.

Although a coat of wax can be applied to give the finish a softer look and feel, I generally avoid using furniture waxes over film-forming finishes. One of the reasons I use film finishes is that if applied properly they need very little maintenance. Wax may wear off pieces that receive a lot of abuse and may eventually need to be rejuvenated with another coat. I have also found that certain household polishes and cleaners may strip off the wax, leaving behind a blotchy mess.

If you do decide to buff a coat of wax onto your completed project, simply apply it in the same manner as you would over any other finish. While some manufacturers make products designed specifically for their water-based finishes, any furniture wax will work well.

I have one final word on rubbing out finishes. A common complaint I hear is that water-based products don't look and feel like traditional solvent-based finishes. While I would argue that the newest generation of water-based products do a good job of imitating the *appearance* of lacquers and varnishes, I agree that they don't *feel* like them. There are several good-quality water-based products that when applied properly and

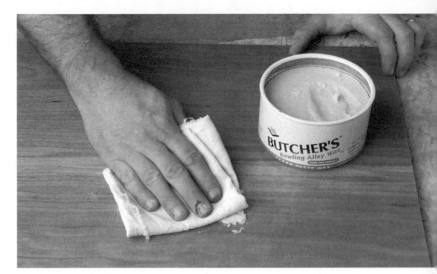

A final coat of wax, though not usually necessary, will give the finish a warmer, softer glow.

rubbed out carefully will look very similar to a nitrocellulose lacquer. However, no matter how much you rub out one of these finishes, it will never have the same feel as a traditional solvent-based product. The reason is simple: The two products are different. The resins used in water-based finishes are different, the solvents are different, and the additives are different. This does not mean they are any better or worse than traditional lacquers, just different.

Whether someone likes the way water-based finishes feel is entirely a matter of personal preference. I suspect that as increasing demand for these products fuels new technologies, water-based finishes will become more and more like solvent-based coatings in most every aspect, including how they feel. Don't be disappointed if your painstakingly applied and hand-rubbed water-based finish feels different from lacquer. If you want something to *feel* like lacquer, you should use lacquer in the first place.

10

Cleaning Up

Whether you are using brushes or spray equipment, the steps involved in cleaning water-based finishes are the same as those for solvent-based coatings. You must be thorough and follow the correct procedures no matter what material you have been using. Knowing how to properly clean and maintain your brushes and spray equipment will not only make cleaning up easier but will also give you better results and help your equipment last longer.

Cleaning solvents

The nice thing about working with water-based finishes is you usually don't need any special solvents for cleanup. In most cases, warm, soapy water works just fine. You don't need gloves, expensive fans, or respirators. And once

you're done, dirty water is easy to dispose of. However, if your brush or gun is especially dirty, or has old, dried finish on it, you may need to use something more than plain water. I have found that with spray equipment I usually use a combination of warm water to clean the loose or wet finish and lacquer thinner for the tougher-to-remove dried material.

Although cleaning spray equipment often generates some dirty lacquer thinner or denatured alcohol, the amount is insignificant when compared with that created when cleaning up after using traditional varnishes and lacquers. The amount of toxic solvents needed to use water-based finishes is so small that the cleanup process is less dangerous and more pleasant than when cleaning up after solvent-based materials.

With water-based products you don't need any of the smelly, toxic, and flammable solvents shown on the left, just the soap and water on the right.

Cleaning brushes

When I was growing up, it seemed that not a summer went by when I wasn't helping some family member paint something. Whether it was a bedroom, house, or old barn, I always had the same attitude: Finish the job as quickly as possible. I came to view paintbrushes as simple tools with limited life spans. As far as I was concerned, the only thing that mattered was that the brushes were clean enough to use until the job was finished. Since I never actually bought a brush with my own money, I viewed them as relatively inexpensive parts of the job that were, in essence, disposable.

When I first began professional woodworking, I still had the attitude that brushes were expendable and weren't worth much time and attention. For the first few years, I bought cheap brushes and had no problem throwing them out when they stopped performing as they should. After all, I reasoned, a few dollars for a new brush was a relatively small expense when compared with the time and material already spent on a job.

Which brush would you rather use? A well-cared-for brush not only lasts longer but is also easier to use and gives better results.

It didn't take me long to figure out why my professional painter friends were so fanatical about cleaning and caring for their brushes. The already small (and often nonexistent) profits I was making as a cabinetmaker had to be increased if I hoped to be successful. As I began to examine my costs, I quickly realized that I was spending more money on paintbrushes than was necessary.

You can buy wire brushes (right) that are specially designed for cleaning paintbrushes, or you can use a general purpose mason's brush (left).

CLEANING A BRUSH

Wiggling the bristles of a brush back and forth will loosen any finish stuck between them and will help break up material dried in the butt of the brush.

From that point forward, I began to look at them differently. I no longer ran out at the start of a new project and bought a cheap brush. Instead, I purchased a variety of good-quality brushes, each suited for a different job. I also began to pay more time and attention to the cleaning process, being sure that at the

end of each day the brushes looked as close to new as possible. I may have spent more money in the short term, but over the long run I have saved a bundle. In fact, I have not had to buy a new brush for more than five years.

Proper cleaning of a brush begins before you even start to use it. It is a good idea to thoroughly wet the brush with clean water before working with water-based products. Wetting the bristles first will help keep the finish from drying on the brush, particularly near the butt, and make it much easier to clean.

The sooner you begin the cleaning process after you are done applying the finish the better. Water-based products dry very quickly, and it is much easier to remove wet paint or lacquer than dry. If you can't clean the brush immediately, place it in something that will keep it wet. This can be the can of finish, a jar of warm, soapy water, or even a tightly sealed plastic bag. The main thing is to keep the brush from drying out before you have time to clean it.

The first step in the cleaning process is to remove as much of the unused finish as possible. Begin by scraping the brush on the side of a can or bucket until no more liquid is being removed. Next, rinse the brush under warm running water, again until no visible finish is coming off. The length of time this takes will depend on how long you were using the brush and how heavy the finish material is. If you were brushing a clear finish on a small item, the rinsing time won't be very long. However, if you were applying latex paint to the side of a house for an entire afternoon, you may have to rinse the brush for quite awhile.

If you were using a heavy-bodied material like latex paint, you should next lay the brush on a flat surface and use a wire brush to scrape as much material as possible off of the bristles. If the finish you were brushing is more viscous, you probably won't need to scrape the bristles with the brush.

After you have scraped the brush, rinse it again with warm water to remove the loosened material. Next, while holding the handle in one hand, grab all of the bristles with your other hand and wiggle them firmly back and forth several times. This will help break up finish that is stuck between the bristles and in the butt of the brush. Rinse the brush again, pointing the bristles straight up into warm running water. This will remove any remaining loosened finish while cleaning material out of the ferrule.

Finally, a fully cleaned brush must be dried before it can be properly stored. Drying a brush is simply a matter of spinning it several times. You can buy a tool, appropriately called a brush spinner, that will do this for you. If you don't have a brush spinner, place the brush handle between your palms and

spin the bristles dry by rubbing your hands together.

The last thing to consider when cleaning a brush is how you are going to store it. An improperly stored brush will lose its shape quickly, making it harder to use. Wrapping the bristles in a paper or cardboard cradle will help prevent this from happening. A good-quality brush should come with a cardboard wrapper

A brush spinner is a fancy gadget that gets clean brushes dry, but all you really need to do is place the brush between your palms and spin it back and forth a few times.

If your brush doesn't have a cardboard wrapper like the one on the left, make a protective covering from heavy paper.

that fits around the bristles. If you don't have this protective sheath, you can use kraft paper or several layers of newspaper. Wrap the paper around the bristles, being careful not to squeeze or distort them, and seal the package with some string or a rubber band. I like to hang my brushes by the handle, but you can also store them on a shelf or in a drawer. If you do lay them down, the important thing to remember is that they should be on a flat surface with nothing under, next to, or on top of them. Placing brushes in a drawer filled with screwdrivers and wrenches guarantees that they will eventually lose their shape.

Cleaning spray equipment

In principle, cleaning a spray gun is just like cleaning a brush: The cleaner you get it today, the better it will work tomorrow. It is true that keeping a spray gun clean requires more work than that for brushes. However, if you follow a few simple guidelines, cleaning doesn't have to be a tedious chore.

The cleaner your spray equipment is, the easier it is to use and the better the results. That is why a thorough cleaning at the end of each day is important. But I would be willing to bet that if you use a spray gun regularly, at some point, whether by choice or accident, you will go home at the end of the day with a dirty, half-full gun still hanging in the spray booth. Fortunately, as long as your cup or pot remains sealed, the finish will not dry in the material container. In fact, when I am spraying large amounts of the same material over several days, I regularly leave the 2½-gallon pressure tank filled overnight, ready to spray the next morning. Leaving material in the cup or pot won't ruin the gun, but it will make it harder to clean the next day.

CLEANING TOOLS
Before beginning the cleanup, you should have a selection of appropriate cleaning tools on hand. Because several pieces of a typical spray gun are machined to tight tolerances, they should never come into contact with hard or sharp objects. In particular, the fluid needle, tip, and air cap must be treated as delicate parts. Scraping off dried paint with a wire brush or nail could scratch the fluid needle or change the shape of the opening in the fluid tip, either of which would cause the gun to leak. Also, picking at the holes in an air cap with a sharp object could deform them, which would distort the fan pattern.

Any cleaning tools that come into contact with a spray gun should be stiff enough to remove dried finish but not hard enough to damage the gun. Most gun manufacturers sell cleaning kits that include an appropriate brush. I have found that a toothbrush works just as well, although it may not last as long. I also keep plenty of toothpicks on hand for picking specks of finish out of hard to reach areas, such as deep inside the horns of an air cap. Finally, a clean, soft rag is needed to wipe down the outside of the gun and any removable parts.

CLEANING GUNS WITH ATTACHED FLUID CUPS
No matter what type of spray system you use, begin the cleaning process by turning off the air supply to the gun. Shooting the gun into an empty container or bucket will remove any air and fluid left in the lines. Also, if you are using a pressurized quart cup, you must be sure to relieve the pressure inside the

container by opening the pressure-relief valve. Failure to do so may cause the paint to splurt all over when you open the cup.

Once all of the air and fluid pressure has been released, remove the gun from the cup and hang the handle over the edge of a can so any finish remaining in the fluid tube can drip out. While the gun is draining, clean the quart cup by thoroughly rinsing it with warm water. Since anything left inside the cup will have to pass through the gun during the next stage of cleaning, it makes sense to get it as clean as possible now. Adding a small amount of dish soap or ammonia to the water will help clean the gun faster but isn't absolutely necessary.

Next, move on to the inside of the cup lid and the lid gasket. Pay particular attention to the gasket and area around the edge of the lid. If the gasket gets very dirty, it may harden or crack, making a tight seal impossible.

When the cup and lid are clean, you are ready to wash the gun itself. Fill the cup one-third to one-half full with warm water and spray it through the gun just as you would any finish material. Continue spraying water through the gun until is comes out clean, which may mean refilling the cup once or twice.

If your gun wasn't particularly dirty, the water sprayed through the tip may have cleaned any dried finish off the air cap as well. However, more often than not, the air cap must be removed and cleaned with a wet brush. In some cases, it may help to soak the cap in a jar of clean lacquer thinner for a few minutes. It is important to remove any obstructions from all of the holes in the air cap, otherwise the next time you use your gun the cap may not atomize the material properly or form a decent spray

A dirty, poorly maintained spray gun, such as the one on the right, will be hard to use and will often give less than desired results.

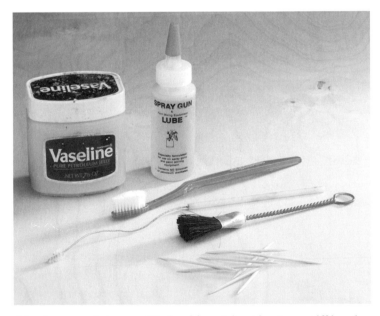

A basic gun maintenance kit should contain at least one stiff brush, some toothpicks, and an appropriate lubricant.

If the rubber gasket is not kept clean, such as the one on the right, you might not be able to get a tight seal between the lid of the gun and the material container.

pattern. Toothpicks come in especially handy for picking specks of dried finish out of the deep holes in an air cap.

Finally, take a clean, damp rag and wipe off the outside of the gun. Although keeping the outside clean may not seem to have a direct effect on how the inside works, it is a good idea to keep it as clean as possible. Dried finish builds on the outside of a gun rather quickly and creeps into places you would not expect. It is a lot easier to remove fresh residue at the end of each day than it is to clean off several weeks' buildup at one time.

If your gun is really dirty or hasn't been thoroughly cleaned in awhile, you may have to take it apart and soak all of the pieces in lacquer thinner. Most guns are easy to disassemble, and some are designed so that even the handle comes apart. If you do have to clean each piece of your gun individually, be sure to remove any rubber O-rings first.

Lacquer thinner does a good job of dissolving most dried finishes, but it wreaks havoc with rubber parts. An O-ring or gasket soaked in lacquer thinner for even the shortest time will swell up well beyond its normal size. Although the piece will eventually shrink, you will not be able to use it until it does. Also, lacquer thinner will dry out a rubber gasket or O-ring to the point where it becomes brittle and can easily crack or break.

Once the gun is clean, reassemble the air cap and place the lid back on the cup. Storing your gun with the air cap in place will protect the expensive needle and tip from any damage if the gun is dropped or banged into something hard. Storing your gun fully assembled will also help keep dirt, dust, and other potential contaminants out of the cup.

CLEANING REMOTE PRESSURE POTS

The only difference between cleaning a remote pressure-feed system and a gun with an attached cup is that with a remote fluid container you must clean the fluid line as well. The easiest way to do this is by blowing any material left in the lines back into the fluid container before cleaning the pot and gun.

Begin by draining the pressure out of the material container and opening the lid. Loosen the air cap retaining ring on the tip of the gun by about a quarter of a turn, then place a rag firmly over the end of the gun. With the atomizing air supply on, trigger the gun until all of the fluid in the line is forced back into the material container.

Once the fluid line has been purged, clean the pressure pot and gun in the

Gun maintenance and water-based coatings

If you work with water-based finishes, your spray equipment should be plastic or stainless steel. If not, parts that come into contact with the water-based product may begin to corrode over time. However, that does not mean that if your equipment is not stainless or plastic you cannot spray water-based finishes. You can still work with these products as long as you thoroughly remove any traces of water after the gun has been cleaned. Blowing off the entire gun and material container with a good blast of clean, dry compressed air is one way to get it dry. If you don't have an air compressor, you can still dry out the interior of the gun by running a few ounces of denatured alcohol through the system as the last step in the cleaning process.

If you spray both water-based finishes and conventional lacquer through the same gun, you must take additional precautions during cleaning. Water-based finishes can dissolve dried lacquer or lacquer thinner, just as lacquer will dissolve water-based residue left in the gun. A simple method to ensure that you don't have problems when switching between the two types of finish involves a three-step line-purging sequence. When switching from solvent to water-based products, first clean the gun with lacquer thinner. Next, run some denatured alcohol through the system, then follow with water. When switching back to traditional lacquer, reverse the sequence. Following this process should eliminate any problems you may encounter while allowing you to spray a variety of finish materials through the same equipment.

same way you would for a gun with an attached cup. Clean the tank first, then run solvent through the gun. It is also a good idea to purge the lines of any remaining solvent by blowing the liquid back into the pot after the gun is clean.

Since you are cleaning the fluid line as well as the gun, cleaning a pressure pot will require substantially more time and solvent than a gun with the cup attached to the handle.

MAINTAINING SPRAY GUNS

Once your gun is clean, be sure to lubricate all of the moving parts. The lubricant you use should be designed for spray equipment and contain no silicone. Silicones are contaminants that ruin finishes by creating crater-like depressions known as fisheye. Once silicone has been introduced into your spray gun, it is difficult to remove, so be careful of what type of lubricants you use both in and around your equipment. A good spray gun should come with at least a small tube of the appropriate lubricant, and most paint stores or auto-body shops will carry it as well. If you run out or can't find a local supplier, try using petroleum jelly—it may be a bit harder to get into tight areas but generally it will do the job.

Appendix 1: Troubleshooting

No matter how skilled you are at applying finishes, problems are bound to occur from time to time. Clean equipment, properly prepared material, good application techniques, and ideal weather conditions are all critical for success when working with water-based products.

The first step to solving any finishing problem is recognizing what went wrong. Determining the cause is often a bit harder, but it gets easier with practice and experience. Fortunately, solving problems is usually a matter of making a few simple adjustments to one or more factors.

The following chart is designed to take the mystery out of solving water-based finishing problems. No doubt you will recognize many of these, for all finishes share some common characteristics. However, several of the problems listed here are unique to water-based products. First, I identify and decribe each problem, then I give a brief list of the potential causes of that problem, including a notation if the problem is specific to a certain type of application equipment. Finally, I offer solutions.

Problem	Cause	Solution
Runs, drips, sags.	Coats are going on too thick.	Apply lighter coats.
	Finish is too thin.	Reduce amount of thinner or add more finish to spray pot.
	Improper spray technique.	Move gun farther away from surface; increase speed of hand motion; hold gun perpendicular to target; use quicker triggering action.
	Brush is being dragged over sharp corners or edges.	Finish brushstroke by moving brush away from, rather than into, sharp corners and edges. Use lighter stroke to feather edges. Load brush with less material. Take final, light pass to tip off finish.

Problem	Cause	Solution
Microbubbles dry in finish, forming a milky or cloudy haze. Unique to spray guns.	Material is atomizing too finely.	Reduce atomization air pressure.
	Material is drying too fast.	Add appropriate retarder.
	Defoamer is no longer working.	Discard finish that is more than 1 year old.
Bubbles in finish.	Defoamer is no longer working.	Discard old finish or add tiny amount of lacquer thinner, mineral spirits, milk, or half-and-half.
	Finish was shaken, not stirred.	Let finish settle in can until bubbles disappear.
	Overworking the finish with excessive brushing.	Flow finish on in long, smooth strokes and leave it alone.
Finish blisters or peels.	Finish is not compatible with undercoating.	Allow undercoating to dry longer or use appropriate sealer between coats.
	Wrong thinner is being used.	Use thinner recommended by manufacturer.
	Spray lines are contaminated.	Clean gun with lacquer thinner, then denatured alcohol, and flush lines with clean water.
	Coats are applied too heavily or without enough drying time.	Apply thinner coats; allow more drying time.
	Temperature of finish or surrounding air is too low.	Warm the finish, the piece being finished, and the finishing room.
	Finish has been frozen.	Discard frozen finish.
Finish pulls dye off of wood. Unique to brushes.	Dye is being redissolved by water in finish.	Apply a washcoat of sealer over dye.
Pigmented primer or topcoat is lumpy or chalky.	Finish is old and additives have settled out of solution or finish has been frozen.	You can try to add thinner and stir thoroughly, but in most cases it is best to throw out the finish and start anew.

Troubleshooting (continued)

Problem	Cause	Solution
Orange peel. Unique to spray guns.	Insufficient atomization pressure.	Increase atomization air pressure.
	Finish viscosity is too thick.	Add appropriate thinner.
	Finish is applied too thinly.	Apply thicker coats.
	Gun is held too far from surface.	Move gun closer to surface.
	Finish, surface being finished, or air in finishing room is too cold to allow proper flow and leveling of finish.	Warm finish by placing it in a bucket of hot water; heat up room prior to finishing.
	Finish is drying too fast.	Add appropriate retarder; reduce atomization air pressure; move gun closer to surface.
Finish appears mottled or textured. Unique to spray guns.	Coating is applied too heavily.	Spray thinner coats, allow more drying time.
	Material is too thin.	Reduce amount of thinner.
	Gun held too close to surface, called "pushing" a finish.	Hold gun farther from surface; decrease air pressure (compressed-air systems).
	Air movement is too strong, called "pulling" a finish.	Move piece being finished farther away from exhaust fan or move portable fans away from piece.
Finish is solidified in can.	Finish is either extremely old or has frozen.	Throw out finish and start over.
Finish won't flow.	Material is too thick.	Add appropriate thinner.
	Coats applied too thin.	Spray thicker coats or apply more finish to brush.
	Finish is old.	Throw out finish and start with new can.
	Not atomized finely enough (spray guns).	Increase atomization air pressure.
	Finish or surrounding air is too cold.	Warm finish or heat finishing room.

Problem	Cause	Solution
Finish takes too long to dry.	Coats applied too thick and too soon.	Apply thinner coats; wait longer between applying coats.
	Too much thinner.	Decrease amount of thinner used.
	Humidity is too high.	Use a dehumidifier in finish room or increase air movement over piece as it dries. Otherwise, wait for drier day to apply finish.
	Air or finish is too cold.	Warm finish or heat finishing room.
Witness lines.	Top layer of finish is cut through by oversanding or rubbing out, leaving a shadow or visible seam between coats.	Make last coat thicker than normal by applying one heavy coat or several very thin coats in rapid succession (works best with spray guns).
Black spots appear in finish after it is dry.	Steel wool particles left in wood begin to rust.	Never use steel wool before applying water-based finishes.
Tip of spray gun clogs.	Small amounts of finish build up on end of gun, restricting amount of fluid that can pass through tip.	Periodically remove dried finish from fluid tip with toothpick or fingernail. Placing a wet rag over tip of gun or placing tip of gun in cup of water when not in use may also help. Coat tip of gun with lubricant. Hold gun farther from surface to reduce bounceback.
Excessive brush or lap marks.	Overbrushing finish.	Use long, smooth strokes to flow finish on.
	Working too slowly or not working from a wet edge.	Work quickly, always maintaining a wet edge.
Finish looks bland, lifeless, or washed out.	Clarity and bluish tint characteristic of water-based products often does not impart the warmth, color, and tone of traditional lacquers and varnishes.	Use sanding sealer or 1-lb. washcoat of shellac before applying topcoat. Sealer or topcoat can also be tinted with small amounts of universal tints or water-soluble dyes.
Colored specks appear in finish. Unique to spray guns.	The gun is not clean and the water-based finish is loosening old paint or pigmented lacquer.	Clean gun with lacquer thinner, followed by denatured alcohol and then water.

Troubleshooting (continued)

Problem	Cause	Solution
Fisheye, a small circular depression in the finish.	Wood contains silicone or wax.	Clean surface with mineral spirits and apply appropriate sealer.
	Spray gun is contaminated with oil.	Spray several light-mist coats over contaminated area. Add manufacturer-recommended fisheye eliminator to finish.
		Clean gun and keep it away from oil and lubricants that contain silicone. Clean or install oil separator on compressed-air line.
Cratering.	Solid particles, often stearates left behind by sandpaper, trapped in surface of finish.	Sand out defect (avoid sandpaper that contains stearates), wipe down surface with damp rag, and recoat.
Dry spray, which is coarse, lumpy texture that looks and feels like fine sandpaper.	Atomization pressure too high.	Decrease atomization pressure.
	Material too thick to atomize properly.	Add appropriate thinner.
	Too much thinner causes coats to dry too fast.	Reduce thinner.
	Gun is moving too fast or is held too far from surface.	Move gun slowly and hold it closer to surface to get a thicker, wetter coat.
Brush won't hold shape.	Wrong type of brush.	Use synthetic-bristle brushes.
	Brush has been improperly cleaned or stored.	After each use, clean and dry brush thoroughly and store it in protective wrapper flat on shelf or hanging on hook.
Bumpy, rough, or coarse surface.	Dirt or dust is in finish or on surface being finished.	Strain finish into clean container before using. Clean finishing area and wipe down piece being finished with damp rag.
	The finish is old.	Discard old finish.
Finish comes out in blobs or foamy strands that look like marshmallow fluff. Unique to spray guns.	There is lacquer thinner in the gun or fluid line.	Clean gun by washing it with lacquer thinner, followed by denatured alcohol and then water.

Appendix 2: Finishing Schedules

The following finishing schedules outline the basic procedures I use in my shop. The schedules are meant to serve as guidelines for several common finishes. The techniques can be adjusted or adapted to suit different materials, equipment, and personal preferences.

Clear finish over oil-based pigmented stain

Although I avoid oil-based products, there are times when I must use pigmented stains. Water-based coatings have improved greatly over the past few years, and in most cases there won't be any adhesion problems over a fully cured oil-based product. However, because I am usually under pressure to finish things as quickly as possible, I often can't wait for the stain to cure. To be safe, I apply a washcoat of shellac between the stain and the topcoat.

1. Sand the piece to 220 grit and remove all dust by blowing off the piece with compressed air.
2. Flood a heavy coat of stain over the surface with a rag or brush. Let the stain sit for 1 to 2 minutes, then wipe off the excess with a clean rag.
3. Let the stain dry overnight, then apply a coat of shellac. It doesn't matter whether you use a 1- or 2-pound cut as long as the shellac has no wax in it and you apply a full coat that covers the entire piece evenly.
4. Let the shellac dry for about 1 hour, then sand with 240-grit wet/dry paper. Sand enough to remove all raised grain, blemishes, and brush marks but not so much that you cut through the shellac into the stain.
5. Wipe off the dust with a slightly damp cloth. At this point, the surface should be fully sealed and appear smooth and a bit shiny. If you see any rough or dull spots, you may need to apply another coat of shellac.
6. Apply the first coat of clear finish fairly lightly and allow it to dry thoroughly before sanding or applying additional coats. Under ideal conditions, the first coat should be dry enough to sand in about 2 hours.

7. Sand the first coat with 320-grit paper and remove all dust with a damp rag before applying the second topcoat. Additional coats can be applied in the same way. As long as you apply subsequent coats within a reasonable time period (8 to 12 hours), sanding is only necessary if the previous coat feels rough or contains dust.

Clear finish over pore filler and dye

The finest finishes consist of pore fillers, dyes and stains, sealers, and clear topcoats, all layered together to form a smooth film that highlights the figure of the wood while giving it rich color and a sense of depth. There are many ways to apply the various elements that make up a truly fine finish. The materials you use and the order in which you apply them depend on your preferences. Following is just one example of how various materials can be combined to create a top-quality finish.

1. Sand the piece with anywhere from 120- to 180-grit paper. Blow all the sanding dust out of the pores with compressed air. If you don't have an air compressor, remove as much dust as possible with a brush, then blow the rest out of the pores with your own lung power.
2. Apply the first coat of dye. This could be the same color as the final finish or a contrasting color.
3. Let the dye dry for 1 to 2 hours, then apply a washcoat of dewaxed shellac in a 1- or 2-pound cut. The shellac will stiffen the grain that was raised by the dye, making it easier to sand.
4. Sand the entire surface with 240-grit wet/dry paper. Apply enough pressure to remove the grain and smooth out the surface, being careful not to cut through the shellac and into the dye. If you do sand through to bare wood, repair the damage by wetting the area with more dye. Let the dye sit for 1 to 2 minutes before wiping off the excess. The spot that was cut through should now blend in with the surrounding area.
5. Once the shellac has been sanded and any cut-throughs repaired, apply the pore filler. If you use a filler that is close in color to the final finish, the pores will blend in. If you use a color that contrasts with the finish, the pores and grain will stand out and be highlighted.

6. Once the filler is dry, sand the surface with 240-grit or finer wet/dry sandpaper. The objective is to remove the filler from the surface of the wood but not from the pores. If the pores are especially deep, you may have to apply a second coat of filler.

7. Seal the filler with another coat of dewaxed shellac. Once the shellac is dry, sand the surface with 320-grit paper. You should now have a surface that is perfectly flat and smooth.

8. If you are happy with the appearance of the surface, you can begin to apply the topcoats. However, in many cases you may want to alter or deepen the color of the finish by applying another coat of dye or even a pigmented stain. If you apply another coat of the same dye, the resulting finish will have a darker, richer color. If you use a different color dye or stain, the wood will contain multiple colors and highlights that seem to come alive when viewed from different angles or under various lighting conditions. You can repeat the dyeing and sealing process as many times as you want until you achieve the desired color.

9. If you do apply additional coats of dye or stain, let them dry, then seal them as before with a washcoat of dewaxed shellac. Once the final coat of shellac is dry, sand the surface with 320-grit paper and remove all the dust with a damp cloth.

10. Apply the first coat of clear finish fairly lightly and allow it to dry for at least 2 hours before any additional coats are applied. At this point, any sanding should be done with a 320-grit or finer paper and is only necessary to remove dust and blemishes. Two coats are all that's needed to protect the wood, but additional coats will add a sense of depth to the finish.

11. For a truly fine finish, rub out the topcoat. The level of gloss you will be able to achieve depends primarily on how long you let the finish cure. A water-based finish can be rubbed out to a soft, satiny sheen after only 2 to 3 days, but a high-gloss shine will be almost impossible. If you do want a gloss finish, let the topcoat cure for at least 7 days before beginning the rubbing process.

Pigmented topcoat

Although I normally use pigmented lacquers for opaque finishes, the following schedule works for latex and acrylic paints as well.

1. Sand the piece to 120 grit, and remove dust from every pore, nook, and cranny with compressed air.
2. Apply a smooth, even coat of primer. Most primers dry fast and should be ready to sand in about 30 minutes.
3. Sand the surface with 240-grit wet/dry paper, and remove all dust with a damp rag. Blow out any cracks or crevices with compressed air.
4. Fill all voids, gaps, holes, and defects with wood putty. Large gaps or seams may need to be filled with caulk.
5. Allow the putty to dry thoroughly before sanding. If you are careful with the putty, you should be able to sand it smooth with 240-grit paper. If you had a lot of large defects to fill, you may have to drop down to a lower grit. The objective is to sand the putty flush with the surrounding wood. In most cases, this will require sanding completely through the primer as well.
6. Spot-prime the putty and all sanded areas first, then immediately apply a second coat of primer to the entire piece.
7. Let the primer dry for 30 to 60 minutes before sanding it smooth. If all is going well, you may try using 320-grit paper, but I find that with primer, finer-grit papers aren't aggressive enough and tend to clog. I usually stick with 240-grit paper throughout the priming process.
8. If the resulting surface is flat, smooth, and free of defects, apply the color coat. If not, repeat steps 4 through 7 as many times as necessary.
9. Once the priming process is complete, remove all dust by wiping the piece with a damp rag.
10. Apply the topcoat as smoothly as possible. Ideally you should only need to apply one coat. However, if the surface is rough or the color uneven, a second coat may be required. Any sanding between these coats should be done very lightly and with a fine paper (320 grit or higher). Deep scratches left in the color coat will be tough to cover and may show through the next coat.
11. If you want to give the finish extra depth and protection or want to change the level of shine, apply a clear coat over the color coat just as you would with any other finish.

Production finish

Following is the schedule I follow when working in production situations where the object is to get a good-quality finish on many pieces as quickly as possible. Although most production situations call for only two coats, you could use this same schedule on fine furniture by simply increasing the number of coats.

1. Sand the piece to 120 grit. The scratch pattern should be even and consistent and running with the grain. Be careful not to leave any swirl marks when using random-orbit sanders.
2. Apply a seal coat. Depending on the brand of finish being used, the seal coat may be either a sanding sealer or the topcoat material itself.
3. Sand the sealer with 240-grit wet/dry paper using an electric palm sander. The drying time of the seal coat depends on the material used and weather conditions. Normally sealer should be ready for sanding in about 30 minutes. On dry days, I have sanded the seal coat in 15 minutes, while on humid days I may have to wait for more than an hour.
4. Remove sanding dust by wiping the piece with a slightly damp rag. Rinse out the rag whenever it becomes dry or loaded with dust.
5. Be sure any moisture left by the rag has evaporated before applying the topcoat. In most production situations, I spray one coat of clear finish over the sealer and I am done. However, on some occasions I may need to apply a second topcoat. If the first coat went on smoothly and there are no blemishes or dust in the finish, I wait 1 to 2 hours before spraying the second coat. If the finish needs sanding, I wait until it is dry, which again could be anywhere from 1 to 2 hours, then sand the surface lightly with 320-grit paper. Finally, I wipe the piece down with a damp rag and spray the next coat.

Glossary

Acrylic Plastic resins that are hard and flexible. Acrylic resins dry clear but are relatively brittle and easy to scratch.

Carrier The liquid portion of a finish in which the resins are suspended or dissolved. The carrier allows the resins to flow freely across the surface being finished.

Coalescing Finish A finish where resins, which are suspended in an emulsion, fuse together as the carrier evaporates. Water-based finishes cure through this process.

Co-solvents Solvents, usually slow-drying alcohols, used in water-based finishes. As the water in the finish evaporates, the co-solvents soften the resins and allow them to stick together (or coalesce).

Cratering Blemishes or depressions left in a finish caused by solid particles trapped under the film. Stearates left behind by sanding are common causes of cratering.

Defoamers Additives used to limit the problem of bubbles in water-based finishes. Defoamers work by breaking the bubbles as soon as they form. The bubbles still exist, but they don't last long enough to cause significant problems.

Dye Small particles of colorant that are dissolved in an appropriate solvent (usually water, alcohol, or lacquer thinner) and used to stain wood. The particles of color are absorbed into the molecular structure of the wood, resulting in deep, even tones.

Evaporative Finish A liquid in which resins form a film as the solvent evaporates. The resins join together without undergoing any chemical changes.

Filler A thick paste containing resins, binders, and solvent that is used to plug the open pores found in wood. The resulting surface is smooth and flat. Fillers may also be used to introduce color contrasts to the grain and are commonly used in the highest-quality finishes.

Fisheye Tiny circular spots, holes, or depressions in a finish, usually caused by a contaminant such as oil, wax, or silicone coming in contact with the surface being finished or the application equipment.

Flatting Agent Finely ground powders that deflect light. Usually added to a finish to control the level of gloss by dulling the shine.

Flow Additive A liquid added to a finish to make the finish easier to spray or brush and to aid its ability to level and form a smooth surface. Most flow additives for water-based finishes are nothing more than water with slow-drying alcohols added.

Hazardous Air Pollutants (HAPs) Chemicals that when released from a drying finish result in the creation of air pollution.

Macrobubbles Relatively large bubbles usually caused by shaking, stirring, or overbrushing the finish. The resulting surface will be rough and bumpy and will require a great deal of sanding.

Melting in (burning in) The process whereby freshly applied lacquer partially redissolves a previous coat. The two coats then fuse together, resulting in one continuous film.

Microbubbles Microscopic bubbles that form in a finish as it is applied with a spray gun. If the finish dries before the bubbles escape, the resulting film may be cloudy, dull, or hazy. The most common cause is too much atomization pressure but may also occur if the defoamer has stopped working.

Nongrain-raising (NGR) dye Water-soluble dyes that contain additives like glycol ether and lacquer thinner. The additives speed up the drying time while reducing or eliminating raised grain. Because they dry so fast, they are usually applied with spray equipment and are most commonly used in production situations.

Orange peel Characteristic of a finish that has not flowed together properly, resulting in a rough, bumpy surface that resembles the skin of an orange. May occur with any type of finish material but only when applied with spray guns.

Overspray Sprayed material that misses the surface being finished and fills the air surrounding the work piece. Often settles back on the piece being finished as dry spray.

Penetrating film finish A liquid that is absorbed into the pores of the wood while also forming a film on the surface. Examples include shellac, nitrocellulose lacquer, and most oil-based varnishes.

Penetrating finish A liquid that is absorbed into the pores of the wood as it dries. Examples include tung and linseed oil.

Pigmented stains A liquid that contains large particles of colorant, binder, and solvent. The particles color the surface of the wood by lodging in open pores and scratches. As the solvent evaporates, the binder holds the particles of colorant in place. The resulting finish highlights contrasting grain but lacks the depth and clarity associated with dyes.

Putty A thick paste consisting of resins, pigments, and solvent, usually used to fill relatively large holes prior to finishing.

Reactive finish A liquid in which the resins undergo a chemical change as the solvent evaporates. The resins link together to form larger molecules through polymerization. Examples include conversion varnishes and tung and linseed oil.

Resins The solid part of a finish that is left behind to form the film as the solvents and additives evaporate. Resins may be natural, such as those found in shellac, or may be man-made acrylics and urethanes found in water-based products.

Retarder A liquid added to a finish to slow down the drying time. Retarders used with water-based products usually contain slow-drying alcohols that help lengthen the open time of the finish, making it easier to apply with a brush or spray equipment on hot, dry days.

Sealer A clear finish that has been altered to make it dry faster and easier to sand. It may also be designed to raise the grain or impart amber color to the wood. As a first coat, sealers fill the pores of the wood while providing a good surface for the next coat to bond to. Sealers may be used to lock defects like grease, wax, or silicone under the finish or as buffers between coats of varying finishes, stains, and dyes.

Shellac A liquid finish that is made from the secretions of a bug found in India and the Far East. The resins are refined to various grades and dissolved with alcohol. Dewaxed shellac makes an excellent sealer under or between just about all finish materials, especially when working with water-based products.

Solids The part of a finish that is left behind when the solvents and additives have fully evaporated (see resins).

Solvent Any material that will dissolve a dried finish.

Surface film finish A liquid that dries on the surface of the piece being finished. Examples include conversion varnish and water-based finishes.

Surfactants Additives found in water-based finishes that are designed to reduce the surface tension of the water, improving the coating's ability to flow and level. Also used to help keep the resins, which would normally be incompatible with water, suspended in the solution.

Tail solvents Relatively slow-drying alcohols used to improve a water-based product's ability to flow and level. They are typically the last additive to evaporate from the finish as it dries.

Thinner A liquid that is added to a finish to lower its viscosity or alter its drying time. Thinners are used to help finishes atomize better when spraying or to make them easier to apply with brushes. Many manufacturers recommend you use a specific flow additive to thin their water-based products, but in most cases clean water works as well.

Universal tinting colors (UTCs) Pigment-laden mixtures used to add color to a finish. Small drops can be added to clear finishes to adjust their hue or to give them a sense of warmth, while larger amounts can be used to tint opaque finishes. Can usually be mixed with any type of finish.

Urethane A plastic resin that is extremely tough and scratch resistant. More expensive than acrylic resins, these are usually found in finishes designed for high-traffic areas such as floors, chairs, and tabletops.

Vinyl sealer A finish made from vinyl modified resins that results in a tough, impenetrable film.

Viscosity A measure of a liquid's resistance to flow. Specifically, it is the measure of the amount of friction between the molecules of the liquid, or how much the liquid sticks to itself.

Viscosity cup A container with a small hole in the bottom used to measure the thickness of a liquid. Timing how long it takes for the fluid to drain through the cup helps determine if the material needs to be thinned prior to spraying.

Volatile organic compounds (VOCs) The hydrocarbons found in solvents that when released into the air react with sunlight to form smog.

Water based A finish that uses water as its primary solvent.

Water borne A solvent-based finish that has been modified to accept water into the emulsion as the primary carrier.

Water reducible A solvent-based finish that has chemicals added to allow it to accept water into the emulsion as a thinner or reducing agent.

Witness lines Shadows or rings that form when one layer of finish is sanded or cut through, exposing the previous coat of finish.

Index

Publisher: JIM CHILDS

Associate Publisher: HELEN ALBERT

Associate Editor: STROTHER PURDY

Editor: DIANE SINITSKY

Layout Artist: SUZIE YANNES

Photographer: ED KELLY

Illustrator: ROSALIE VACCARO

Typeface: PLANTIN, GLYPHA

Paper: 68-LB. STORA G-PRINT

Printer: QUEBECOR PRINTING/HAWKINS, CHURCH HILL, TENNESSEE